DEDICATION

To my daughter, Colette.
You are my world.

CONTENTS

ACKNOWLEDGMENTS

In my experience, every interesting project that has come across my desk has been the result of a shared meal. This one was no different. My first thanks go to my agent and special friend Beth Shepard of Beth Shepard Communications, LLC. She called one day and said, "Let's brainstorm." I got in the car, and a few hours later we were sitting in a café, eating our salads, drinking our tea, and tossing ideas around. My food and wellness coaching practice was well underway with clients suffering from food disorders, along with obesity and diabetes. During my many years as a lecturer and cooking instructor on Asian food and its health benefits (when mindfully prepared), questions about how I maintain a healthy weight and lifestyle as a food professional have always come up. Honestly, I owe it to my Asian upbringing, where balance and tuning into the body are key. Beth and I discussed my approach to teaching people from all walks of life about how to build a healthy, intimate relationship with food and becoming self-aware as a result.

From our conversation, the *Asian Flavors Diabetes Cookbook* was born. Beth approached Abe Ogden, Director of Book Publishing at the American Diabetes Association, to whom I am extremely grateful for instantly recognizing the potential in this project. The ADA did not have an Asian cookbook in their collection. It also made sense because, in Asian culture, the word "food" is synonymous with medicine. Therefore, in making the right choices and combining them in specific ways, food has the ability to help anyone maintain a healthy lifestyle.

I'd also like to thank Rebekah Renshaw, Developmental Editor, for her valuable input in helping shape the book, and to Heschel Falek, Associate Director of Marketing and Publicity, for making sure the book is available to all, and Rikki Campbell Ogden of pixiedesign, llc for her beautiful book design and layout.

I'd also like to thank my friend Chef Shiyam Sundar, whose own mother suffers from diabetes. Well-versed in Asian cuisines with a deep understanding of spices and herbs and their health benefits, his insights and enthusiasm while testing every recipe in this book were invaluable.

As always, I thank my family and friends for their patience. I hope you will forgive my absence due to this wonderful project, and continue to forgive me knowing that this wasn't the last time.

A thousand thanks to all!

Corinne Trang

INTRODUCTION

In Asian cultures, balance is everything. In the kitchen, we're constantly exploring textures and colors. We play with flavor profiles that include sour, bitter, salty, sweet, and spicy notes—the essence of good food. Applying these characteristics to a wide variety of vegetables, fruit, seafood, and meats is part of a centuries-old tradition of using food as preventative medicine.

Based on the idea that food is medicine and medicine is food, Asian food preparation is largely based on the ancient Chinese food philosophies and the concept of balanced opposites known as *yin yang*. With this in mind, the *Asian Flavors Diabetes Cookbook* is filled with recipes that can help you maintain a healthy lifestyle, while eating balanced meals and synthesizing body, mind, and spirit. It is written for the person with diabetes in mind and for friends and family who will, no doubt, want to partake in this delicious affair.

The *Asian Flavors Diabetes Cookbook* is a compilation of simple comfort foods from all over Asia, including classics, such as wontons and fresh spring rolls, as well as contemporary recipes like salads tossed in Asian-inspired dressings. The recipes are nutritionally sound using healthy cooking techniques such as steaming, stir-frying, braising, and grilling, for a wide variety of dishes that will impress your guests. The next time you sit at the table, look at your plate. If it is at least 70% filled with vegetables, you're on your way to maintaining a healthy weight and lifestyle. Included is a chapter focusing on vegetables and fruit, to ensure that your plate always has a rainbow of colors and vitamins.

Transforming simple recipes into elegant fare can be easy. Sometimes, it's as simple as throwing a few sprigs of cilantro, mint, or basil into the dish to make it visually appealing. In no time at all, these dishes will become signatures in your very own kitchen. Living with diabetes, while challenging, can be manageable and guilt-free with these fresh, simple recipes.

This collection of updated recipes inspired by Chinese, Japanese, Korean, and Southeast Asian food cultures will become your "go-to" for Asian-inspired diabetes-friendly meals. Starting with a basic pantry of Asian ingredients, each recipe will be broken down with easy step-by-step instructions as well as menu ideas serving one, two, four, or more. You'll never need to cook a special meal just for yourself. Now your friends and family will share your enthusiasm for Asian flavors and enjoy the same satisfying meal, making it much easier for everyone during mealtime.

Before you flip through the recipe chapters, I encourage you to read *Chapter 1: The Asian Pantry and Basics* chapter introduction, which gives you insight onto the organizing principle of Asian cuisine and its fundamental building blocks. You will quickly find out that Asian cooking requires only a handful of ingredients for creating authentic meals.

I would also like for you to consider cutting back on proteins and filling your plate up with vegetables instead. For example, when creating a meal for six, be sure to select two to three vegetable recipes to serve along one protein (either meat or seafood) and one starch (noodles or rice). Approach every meal this way, and you will feel balanced every time.

Eat well and be well!

CT

CHAPTER ONE
The Asian Pantry and Basics

This is perhaps the most important chapter in the book, giving you insight on the building blocks of Asian flavor profiles. It all starts with building an Asian pantry, which is easy nowadays, especially with basic ingredients readily available in Asian markets, health food stores, international aisles at supermarkets, and mail-order sources on the Internet.

In this chapter you will find basic recipes for marinades, dipping sauces, and stocks—the foundation of Asian cooking. Meals are built one flavor at a time. For example, stir-frying starts with heating oil over high heat. Next, you add the garlic, ginger, and scallion and stir-fry these until fragrant and light golden, seasoning your cooking vessel, such as a wok, in the process. Only then do you add the main ingredients, such as sliced meats, seafood, or vegetables. After a few seconds of stir-frying these until just cooked or wilted, a light drizzling of soy sauce and perhaps some sesame oil is added seconds before transferring to a serving dish. This is stir-frying in a nutshell!

In a braised dish, you will start the same way, first stir-frying the garlic, ginger, and scallion until fragrant and lightly golden, then adding the herbal paste and stir-frying it until a shade darker. Generally, adding a liquid, such as stock, prior to adding the main ingredients, follows this. In a Thai curry dish, it means adjusting the flavor to create a sweet, sour, salty, spicy, and bitter character. To create this balance of flavor, lime or lemon juice is added to the pot, followed by fish sauce and palm sugar to counter balance the spicy curry paste with the mildly bitter herb stir-fry. Coconut milk is often added alone or along with the above-mentioned stock to round out the flavors. One layer at a time, the flavors are integrated to create a balanced meal.

Once you've acquired some understanding of the basic principles, it will be important for you to build a pantry of the most commonly used ingredients. These are used in combination to create the foundation of hundreds of Asian classic and contemporary dishes.

One of the most common and healthful cooking techniques in Asia is stir-frying, which requires high heat and constant tossing of ingredients to distribute the heat evenly throughout to prevent the food from burning during the cooking process. This technique is also quick and gets dinner on the table in minutes, and the ingredients are tossed and cooked with such rapidity that they retain most of their nutrients. For this technique, a good-quality plain cooking oil that does not burn at high temperature is key to tasty results.

OILS AND SAUCES

PEANUT OIL, also known as "groundnut" oil, is the most commonly used cooking oil in Asia. It is ideal for stir-frying and deep-frying.

GRAPESEED OIL is another basic, clean-flavored oil that can be used for high-temperature cooking. It has the same health benefits as olive oil, but generally flavorless in comparison, which is ideal when cooking with spices.

There are FLAVORING OILS also that can be used to enhance any number of dishes. These oils should not be used for direct-heat cooking as a substitute for peanut or grapeseed oils. They should be used in marinades, salad dressings, or dipping sauces, or for last-minute drizzling over meat, seafood, or vegetarian dishes.

DARK OR "TOASTED" SESAME OIL is considered a flavoring condiment that can be used to enhance all sorts of foods. It is amber to dark brown in color and has a strong aroma that will go a long way. Use sparingly!

CHILI OIL is reddish-orange in color and spicy. Oftentimes, it uses either sesame oil or soybean oil as a base. A few drops will do.

SEA SALT is used in Asia for pickling and preserving.

SOY SAUCE AND FISH SAUCE

Soy sauce and fish sauce are used for everyday cooking, such as braising or stir-frying, and are typically the core ingredients to many marinades and dipping sauces. In an effort to reduce the amount of salt in the recipes, "light soy sauce" (a low-sodium alternative to regular soy sauce) is generally called for. Sea salt or low-sodium salt can be used as an alternate seasoning.

LIGHT SOY SAUCE is a low-sodium alternative to regular soy sauce made from fermented soybean-based product. It is used as a main seasoning agent, replacing salt, in Chinese, Korean, and Japanese cooking. Use to season stir-fries, marinades, dipping sauces, or braised or stewed dishes. Caution: soy sauce contains wheat. If you suffer from a wheat allergy, use low-sodium tamari instead, but be sure to read the label, as some tamari sauces also contain wheat.

FISH SAUCE is made from dried anchovy extract. Used in Southeast Asian cuisines including Vietnamese, Malaysian, Filipino, and Thai cooking, for example, select a fish sauce that is amber in color and free from any rock salt formation. For best results, use fish sauce within six months of opening the bottle. The sauce continues to ferment once opened and in contact with air. The older it gets, the darker it gets, and the more salt crystals form at the bottom as the liquid evaporates, and the saltier it is as a result. Fish sauce is not just a salting agent; it is used for its fish essence. Therefore, it is best used up quickly before it gets too old. Buy in small quantities unless you use it regularly. *Tip: Refrigerating it will slow down the fermentation process, and you may be able to use it for up to nine months.* (Technically, fish sauce does not go bad, because it has so much salt in it. However, the flavor is not as clean or desirable when allowed to get too old.)

SEA SALT comes from evaporated sea water. It contains traces of minerals and gets its subtle flavor and color from salt water. It is moist and sticky, because it has not been highly processed like refined salts.

LOW SODIUM SALT is processed and generally contains about 45 to 65% less sodium depending on the brand.

CHILI SAUCES AND HERBAL PASTES

Chili sauces and herbal pastes are used in many cuisines throughout Asia. Some can be used straight from the bottle, or added to dipping sauces or marinades, while others are the backbone of stews, braised dishes, or soups.

SRIRACHA is a smooth and bright red chili-garlic sauce that generally comes in a squirt bottle. It can be added to salad dressings in small quantities and can also be added to dipping sauces, stir-fried noodles, or rice to add a little extra heat.

CHILI-GARLIC SAUCE is chunky, bright red, and excellent when added to soy sauce and served as a dipping sauce for dumplings. It is also excellent when added to marinades in the absence of fresh red Thai chilies.

RED CURRY PASTE is a spicy chili and herb paste, which contains key ingredients, such as lemongrass, kaffir limes leaves, and galangal, all necessary for Thai coconut curries. While the red curry paste is now readily available, also look for green and yellow curry pastes for a different color and intensity.

MISO PASTE is available in too many variations to mention here, but basic ones come in a grainy or smooth texture and are labeled "white," "red," or "black." "White" miso paste is the most popular and mild of the three basic versions. As a general rule, the darker the miso, the saltier it is. Therefore, the "white miso," known by its Japanese name as "shiromiso," is the least salty and has a subtly sweet character. Use in salad dressings or marinades or to make miso soup.

DRY INGREDIENTS

Dry ingredients are popular in Asian cookery, because they are more concentrated in flavor than their fresh counterparts. As a result, the dried versions are used in smaller quantities, making them ideal ingredients for the frugal cook!

DRIED SHITAKE MUSHROOMS are great to

have on hand in your dry pantry. There are many different types of dried shitake mushrooms. Some are thick with whitish caps, while some are thin with dark brown caps. The uniformity in a package will often determine the cost. The more uniform and carefully selected, the more expensive. For the recipes in this book, an inexpensive batch will do. Dried shitakes need to be soaked until fully softened and rehydrated before using. The woody stems are discarded, and the caps either julienned, quartered crosswise, or left whole before adding to stir-fries, stews, or soups. The soaking water can be filtered and used for making stock infused with scallion and ginger as well.

GOJI BERRIES, also known as wolfberries, are bright red berries the size of a small bird's eye. Sweet, slightly bitter, and chewy, they are full of antioxidants and can be added to anything for a splash of color. Goji berries can be inexpensive or expensive, depending on where you purchase them. Asian markets usually carry inexpensive versions, free of fancy packaging.

FIVE-SPICE POWDER is a popular spice blend originating in China, but often used in Vietnamese cooking, especially for marinating meat and poultry. While the dominant flavor is star anise, it also contains cinnamon, cloves, fennel seeds, and Szechuan peppercorns. There are variations, but generally blends imported from China are dominant with star anise, while those made here in the U.S. contain more cinnamon.

INDIAN CURRY POWDER is another spice blend, heavy with turmeric, which gives it its vibrant yellow color. Blends differ from one another but usually include fenugreek, cumin, coriander, red pepper, cloves, mustard seeds, cardamom, caraway, ginger, garlic, and nutmeg. Versatile, it is good to have on hand, for a light sprinkle of curry powder on vegetables or chicken before roasting them to create an easy meal that is a little out of the ordinary. Feel free to add it to chicken salad or use it to flavor rice.

OTHER CONDIMENTS

Some other ingredients worth stocking up on:

UNSEASONED RICE VINEGAR is always good to have on hand. It is not as harsh as white vinegar, and not as sweet as white balsamic or apple vinegar, though the latter makes for an interesting fruity character, which lends itself well to Asia's complex flavor profiles. *Note: Read the label carefully as there are "seasoned" rice vinegars. If using these, you will have to adjust the recipes because these vinegars contain extra salt and sugar.*

LIGHT UNSWEETENED COCONUT MILK is a main ingredient in Southeast Asian cuisines and employed in both sweet and savory dishes. For the sake of keeping the calorie count to a minimum, the recipes call for using low-fat or light unsweetened coconut milk, which is essentially watered-down coconut milk, rendering any dish less creamy but still very flavorful. These usually contain 65% less fat than regular conconut milk. As a substitute, unsweetened almond or rice milk are employed in some recipes to keep the saturated fat count down. Either one will offer a different flavor that is still delicious.

HOISIN SAUCE is a thick dark brown paste derived from soybeans. It is both sweet and salty and is widely used in flavoring dipping sauces and marinades.

PALM SUGAR is derived from coconut palm trees and widely used as the main sweetner in Asian cuisines.

AGAVE NECTAR, derived from the agave plant, the same plant harvested for making tequila, is sweeter than honey, so less will go a long way. It is also more subtle in flavor and easier to blend, making it ideal for using in dipping sauces or marinades, for example. Be sure to look for "100% pure" agave nectar.

BASIC AROMATICS

There are some key basic aromatics that you should always keep in your refrigerator, for they are the backbone to many Asian dishes. They are GARLIC, SCALLIONS, GINGER, LIMES, LEMONS, MINT, and CILANTRO.

Still others will also enhance some of the recipes that follow. They are:

THAI BASIL, with its dark pointy leaves and purple stem, has a licorice-like flavor that is most recognizable in Thai and Vietnamese cooking, among other Southeast Asian cuisines.

THAI CHILIES (fresh or brined) are tiny chilies, generally measuring about 1 inch long, with colors ranging from green, to yellowish-orange, to red. They are about a 9 on the heat scale of 1 to 10. Remove the seeds from the pods before using, for a more subtle, yet powerful heat.

KAFFIR LIMES LEAVES are hard to find, and if you can't, just omit them entirely from the recipe. They are dark, two-part green leaves that resemble the figure "8." They are available fresh, frozen, or dried. Fresh and frozen are the most fragrant, but dried leaves will do in a pinch.

LEMONGRASS STALKS are fairly easy to find nowadays in better "gourmet" supermarkets and lend a citrusy note to any dish. Remove the bruised outer leaves, dark fibrous and dried green tops, and hard root end before using. The white to light green parts, averaging about 10 inches long, can be grated for marinades and sliced or crushed for stews. You can also knot the stalk before adding to stocks or stews, making it easy to remove before serving.

WRAPS

Wraps are also popular in Asia, and they come in all sorts of shapes, sizes, and textures. Some are leaves, while others are made of wheat flour or rice flour. Their role is to hold all sorts of fillings while lending texture and flavor.

GRAPE LEAVES are used in Vietnamese cooking as a substitute for *la lot* leaves, which are used in vietnam for making beef rolls. Grape leaves be found in jars preserved in brine. If you have freshly picked grape leaves, simply poach them in hot water until just wilted, and cool them prior to using in the recipe. Trim off the stems before using.

SPRING ROLL WRAPPERS are light beige in color, square or round, paper thin, somewhat translucent as a result, and stretchy. They are wheat-based and used for making crispy spring rolls, either fried or baked. These can be found in the freezer section of Asian markets.

RICE PAPERS are round in shape and come in 6-, 8-, and 10-inch rounds. Buy the size you need according to the presentation you'd like to have. Rice papers should always be soaked in cold water one at a time, to soften prior to using. They should be flattened and blotted dry with a paper towel or clean kitchen towel to remove excess water (rendering them sticky, not slippery) prior to filling them with ingredients and rolling.

Creating a basic Asian pantry is quite simple; just by having a handful of ingredients like soy sauce, rice vinegar, dark sesame oil, peanut oil, ginger, garlic, and scallions, you can create healthy and simple stir-fries to serve over rice every day.

LEMON-MISO DRESSING

SERVES 15 | SERVING SIZE: 1 TABLESPOON

This Japanese-inspired dressing is versatile and perfect for dressing roasted vegetables, seasoning a cold noodle salad, or simply drizzling over a variety of fresh leafy salad greens. Miso is a fermented soybean paste available in dozens of variations derived from three principle ones, including the most popular and readily available "white" (beige), "red" (brown), and "black" (dark brown). The darker the miso, the saltier it is. Here I use "white" miso, or shiro-miso, which has a sweet note that counterbalances its saltiness. **Tip:** *This makes enough dressing for four large salads.*

2 tablespoons shiro-miso ("white" miso)

2 teaspoons local honey (optional)

1 ounce (1-inch piece) fresh ginger, peeled and finely grated or juiced

1/2 teaspoon sriracha (optional)

Juice of 2 lemons (about 1/3 cup), or 1/3 cup rice vinegar

2 teaspoons sesame oil

1/2 cup grapeseed or peanut oil

1 scallion, trimmed, white and green parts minced

Freshly ground black pepper

1 In a bowl, whisk together the shiro-miso, honey, ginger, sriracha, lemon juice, sesame oil, and grapeseed or peanut oil, until well combined or emulsified. Stir in the scallions, season with black pepper, and serve.

		EXCHANGES/CHOICES
Calories 75	Sodium 45 mg	1 1/2 Fat
Calories from Fat 70	Potassium 20 mg	
Total Fat 8.0 g	Total Carbohydrate 75 g	
Saturated Fat 0.8 g	Dietary Fiber 0 g	
Trans Fat 0.0 g	Sugars 1 g	
Cholesterol 0 mg	Protein 0 g	

WALNUT-MISO SAUCE

SERVES 8 | **SERVING SIZE: 2 TABLESPOONS**

Asian-style salad dressings or sauces are becoming popular, especially in Japanese restaurants. In this version, walnut is added to the sauce for a more nutritious and nuttier version. This sauce can be tossed with fresh salad greens, served over roasted vegetables, or served as a dipping sauce for roasted or grilled meat or seafood. Miso is a soybean paste that can be found in the refrigerated section of health food stores and some supermarkets.

2 tablespoons shiro-miso

1/3 cup chopped walnuts

3 tablespoons rice vinegar

2 tablespoons sake

1/4 cup grapeseed oil or extra virgin olive oil

1-inch piece ginger, peeled and chopped

1 scallion, trimmed and chopped

1 tablespoon local honey, pure maple syrup, or agave nectar (optional)

Freshly ground black pepper

1 In the bowl of a mini food processor, add the shiro-miso, walnuts, rice vinegar, sake, oil, ginger, scallion, honey, and pepper to taste. Process until smooth.

Calories 110	Sodium 85 mg
Calories from Fat 90	Potassium 50 mg
Total Fat 10.0 g	Total Carbohydrate 3 g
Saturated Fat 1.0 g	Dietary Fiber 1 g
Trans Fat 0.0 g	Sugars 1 g
Cholesterol 0 mg	Protein 1 g

EXCHANGES/ CHOICES
2 Fat

HERBAL SOY SAUCE DRESSING

SERVES 6 | SERVING SIZE: 2 TABLESPOONS

Tangy, savory, and spicy, this soy sauce-based dressing can be used as a dipping sauce for dumplings or any number of grilled meats or seafood entrées. Stir-frying basics like ginger, garlic, and cilantro deepen the flavor of this sauce.

1/4 cup light soy sauce

1/4 cup rice vinegar

1 tablespoon local honey or agave nectar (optional)

2 teaspoons dark sesame oil

3 tablespoons grapeseed or peanut oil

2 large garlic cloves, peeled and minced

1 ounce ginger, peeled and finely julienned or minced

1 red Thai chili, seeded and minced or thinly sliced, or 1 teaspoon sriracha (chili-garlic sauce)

12 sprigs cilantro, stems trimmed, chopped

1 In a bowl, add the soy sauce, vinegar, honey, and sesame oil.

2 Meanwhile, heat a skillet over high heat. Add the grapeseed oil, and stir-fry the garlic and ginger until golden, about 30 seconds. Add the chili and cilantro, and continue to stir-fry until just wilted, about 30 seconds more. Transfer the stir-fry, including oil, to the soy sauce mixture. Stir and serve.

Calories 90	Sodium 370 mg
Calories from Fat 70	Potassium 70 mg
Total Fat 8.0 g	Total Carbohydrate 3 g
Saturated Fat 0.9 g	Dietary Fiber 0 g
Trans Fat 0.0 g	Sugars 1 g
Cholesterol 0 mg	Protein 1 g

EXCHANGES/ CHOICES
2 Fat

SPICY FISH SAUCE DRESSING

SERVES 24 | SERVING SIZE: 1 TABLESPOON

This classic Vietnamese dipping sauce or dressing is called nuoc cham. Offering a medley of flavors—sweet, spicy, salty, bitter, and sour—this versatile sauce can be drizzled over a simple bowl of rice, a salad, or grilled, roasted, or steamed seafood or meat. For a mild flavor, slice garlic and chilies. For a more pronounced flavor, mince both.

1/4 cup fish sauce

1/4 cup agave nectar

1/3 cup lime or lemon juice
(about 2 limes or lemons)

1/4 cup filtered water

1 large clove garlic, sliced or minced

2 red Thai chilies, stems and seeds removed, sliced or minced

1 In a medium bowl, whisk together the fish sauce, agave nectar, lime juice, water, garlic, and chilies. Let stand for 30 minutes, allowing the flavors to blend, before serving.

Calories 15
Calories from Fat 0
Total Fat 0.0 g
Saturated Fat 0.0 g
Trans Fat 0.0 g
Cholesterol 0 mg

Sodium 455 mg
Potassium 25 mg
Total Carbohydrate 3 g
Dietary Fiber 0 g
Sugars 3 g
Protein 0 g

EXCHANGES/ CHOICES
Free food

SPICY PEANUT SAUCE

SERVES 16 | SERVING SIZE: 2 TABLESPOONS

Popular in the cuisines of Southeast Asia, peanut sauce is versatile and commonly eaten with grilled pork meatballs or fresh spring rolls. It is also delicious with pan-crisped tofu and any number of grilled seafood or meats. Refrigerate for up to 3 days or freeze for up to 3 months.

1 tablespoon grapeseed or peanut oil

1 tablespoon red Thai curry paste

1/2 cup unsalted roasted peanuts, finely ground

2 tablespoons palm sugar or agave nectar

1/2 cup light unsweetened coconut milk

1 1/2 cups Basic Asian Chicken Stock (page 17), or store-bought low-sodium chicken stock

1 tablespoon fish sauce

1 1/2 tablespoons hoisin sauce

1/4 cup freshly squeezed lime juice (about 1 1/2 to 2 limes)

8 fresh cilantro sprigs, stems trimmed, and minced

1 In a small saucepan, heat the oil over medium heat, and stir-fry the curry paste until fragrant, about 1 minute. Add the peanuts, and continue to stir-fry until two shades darker but not burnt, about 8 minutes. Add the palm sugar or agave nectar, coconut milk, stock, fish sauce, and hoisin sauce. Reduce heat to low, and simmer until sauce is slightly thickened, about 20 minutes.

2 Remove from heat, stir-in the lime juice and cilantro, and serve hot or at room temperature.

Calories 70
  Calories from Fat 45
Total Fat 5.0 g
  Saturated Fat 1.3 g
  Trans Fat 0.0 g
Cholesterol 0 mg

Sodium 160 mg
Potassium 95 mg
Total Carbohydrate 4 g
  Dietary Fiber 1 g
  Sugars 3 g
Protein 2 g

EXCHANGES/ CHOICES
1/2 Carbohydrate
1 Fat

CITRUS SOY SAUCE DRESSING

SERVES 22 | **SERVING SIZE: 2 TABLESPOONS**

Inspired by the classic Japanese "ponzu" sauce, this sweet, salty, and tangy dressing is a perfect complement to grilled meat or seafood. The sharpness of the lemon brings balance to any rich protein. Use it as a dipping sauce, marinade, or basting liquid. It can be made weeks ahead of time and can be kept refrigerated.

1 cup light soy sauce

3/4 cup sake

Juice of 3 lemons (about 1/2 cup)

3 tablespoons agave nectar or pure maple syrup

1/4 cup rice vinegar

4 garlic cloves, crushed and peeled

3 scallions, trimmed and crushed

1-inch piece fresh ginger, thinly sliced

One 2 × 4-inch square piece kombu (kelp), wiped

1 In a large bowl, whisk together the soy sauce, sake, lemon juice, agave nectar, and rice vinegar. Add the garlic, scallions, and ginger, and kombu. Mix well and let stand at room temperature for 12 hours or overnight. Discard solids, and transfer sauce to a jar and refrigerate until ready to use.

Calories 30
  Calories from Fat 0
Total Fat 0.0 g
  Saturated Fat 0.0 g
  Trans Fat 0.0 g
Cholesterol 0 mg

Sodium 405 mg
Potassium 40 mg
Total Carbohydrate 0 g
  Dietary Fiber 2 g
  Sugars 1 g
Protein 15 g

EXCHANGES/ CHOICES
1/2 Carbohydrate

SPICY SOY SAUCE MARINADE

SERVES 5 | SERVING SIZE: 1 TABLESPOON

Every Asian cook has a soy sauce marinade that uses basic Asian pantry ingredients, such as ginger, garlic, scallion, soy sauce, and dark sesame oil. It can be made in advance, refrigerated, and used as a marinade or to season stir-fries. *Note: You only need enough marinade to coat meat. There is enough here for up to 1 pound of protein. Use this marinade freshly made for optimal flavor, or refrigerate for up to 1 week. Use 1 1/2 to 2 tablespoons of sauce to stir-fry up to 8 ounces of protein.*

1/4 cup light soy sauce

1 tablespoon agave nectar

1 teaspoon dark sesame oil

1 large garlic clove, peeled and minced

1 scallion, trimmed and minced

1 tablespoon grated ginger

1 teaspoon sriracha (chili-garlic sauce)

1 In a bowl, add the soy sauce, agave nectar, sesame oil, garlic, scallion, ginger, and sriracha.

Calories 30	Sodium 435 mg
Calories from Fat 10	Potassium 40 mg
Total Fat 1.0 g	Total Carbohydrate 4 g
Saturated Fat 0.1 g	Dietary Fiber 0 g
Trans Fat 0.0 g	Sugars 3 g
Cholesterol 0 mg	Protein 1 g

EXCHANGES/ CHOICES
1/2 Carbohydrate

FIVE-SPICE FISH SAUCE MARINADE

SERVES 8 | SERVING SIZE: 1 TABLESPOON

Marinades play a big role in Asian cuisines; this sweet and savory sauce compliments chicken, pork, and duck. Marinate meats for 30 minutes before stir-frying, grilling, or roasting. This is my go-to marinade when making chicken kebobs. *Note: You only need enough marinade to coat meat.*

2 tablespoons fish sauce

2 tablespoons filtered water

2 tablespoons agave nectar

1/2 teaspoon Chinese five-spice powder

1 tablespoon grapeseed or peanut oil

1 large garlic clove, peeled and minced (about 2 teaspoons)

1/2 ounce ginger, peeled and minced (about 1 tablespoon)

1 In a bowl, stir together the fish sauce, water, agave nectar, five-spice powder oil, garlic, and ginger. Use immediately for optimal flavor, or refrigerate up to one week.

Calories 30	**Sodium** 345 mg
Calories from Fat 15	**Potassium** 20 mg
Total Fat 1.5 g	**Total Carbohydrate** 4 g
Saturated Fat 0.2 g	**Dietary Fiber** 0 g
Trans Fat 0.0 g	**Sugars** 3 g
Cholesterol 0 mg	**Protein** 0 g

EXCHANGES/ CHOICES
1/2 Fat

ASIAN CHICKEN STOCK

SERVES 12 | SERVING SIZE: 1 CUP

Making Asian Chicken stock is worth every minute. It requires five ingredients, and the chicken meat can be used to make Minty Jasmine Rice with Chicken (page 62). It's a two-for-one deal! When making stock, be sure to simmer rather than boil, so the stock remains clear.

2 1/2 pounds chicken, skin removed

6 scallions, trimmed and halved crosswise

4 ounces ginger, thinly sliced

1 tablespoon fish sauce

1 teaspoon black peppercorns

1. In a large stockpot, combine all the ingredients, and cover with 6 quarts water. Bring to a boil over high heat. Reduce heat to a simmer, and cook until the chicken is done, about 2 hours.

2. Transfer the chicken to a plate, and remove the meat, shredding it and reserving it for other recipes. Return the bones to the stockpot, and continue to simmer until the liquid has reduced by half, about 2 hours more. Let cool and strain the stock. Discard the solids.

3. Refrigerate until the fat has solidified enough to remove. Divide into 1-quart containers, and refrigerate for up to 3 days, or freeze for up to 3 months.

VARIATION

Substitute a 4-pound slab of pork ribs for the chicken, and proceed with recipe, simmering the stock for four hours with both meat and bones.

Calories 10
  Calories from Fat 0
Total Fat 0.0 g
  Saturated Fat 0.1 g
  Trans Fat 0.0 g
Cholesterol 5 mg

Sodium 125 mg
Potassium 15 mg
Total Carbohydrate 0 g
  Dietary Fiber 0 g
  Sugars 0 g
Protein 1 g

EXCHANGES/ CHOICES
Free food

SCALLION-GINGER SALT DIP

SERVES 16 | SERVING SIZE: 1 TABLESPOON

This sharp scallion, ginger, and sea salt dip is often served with steamed chicken in Chinese restaurants. It is absolutely delicious and not overwhelming at all, though bold. A small dab will go a long way. While it is traditionally served with chicken, this dip is also delicious with roasted or grilled pork. This sauce keeps well refrigerated, but it always tastes better made fresh.

1/2 cup finely grated ginger

12 scallions, trimmed and minced

1–2 teaspoons low-sodium salt

1/3 cup grapeseed or vegetable oil

1 In a bowl, stir together all the ingredients until well combined. Use immediately, or refrigerate for up to 1 week.

Calories 45
  Calories from Fat 40
Total Fat 4.5 g
  Saturated Fat 0.4 g
  Trans Fat 0.0 g
  Cholesterol 0 mg

Sodium 360 mg
Potassium 45 mg
Total Carbohydrate 1 g
  Dietary Fiber 0 g
  Sugars 0 g
  Protein 0 g

EXCHANGES/ CHOICES
1 Fat

FRIED GARLIC OIL

SERVES 24 | SERVING SIZE: 1 TEASPOON

Flavored oils are incredibly versatile, and this Fried Garlic Oil is perfect used as a cooking oil or drizzled over salads. In Asia, fried garlic is often used as a garnish for a variety of soups.

1/3 cup vegetable oil

2 heads garlic, crushed, peeled, and minced

1 In a small skillet over medium heat, add the oil and garlic. When it starts sizzling, stir continuously until the garlic is lightly golden throughout, about 3 minutes. Turn off the heat, and let stand until golden. Cool and transfer garlic with oil to a jar. Refrigerate for up to 1 week.

Calories 30	Sodium 0 mg
Calories from Fat 25	Potassium 10 mg
Total Fat 3.0 g	Total Carbohydrate 1 g
Saturated Fat 0.2 g	Dietary Fiber 0 g
Trans Fat 0.0 g	Sugars 0 g
Cholesterol 0 mg	Protein 0 g

EXCHANGES/ CHOICES
1/2 Fat

FRIED SCALLION OIL

SERVES 8 | SERVING SIZE: 1/4 CUP

Popular in the cuisine of Vietnam, this Fried Scallion Oil is perfect for garnishing rice, tossing with noodles, or drizzling on all sorts of grilled or roasted meats and seafood. Make it in advance and refrigerate for up to 1 week, though freshly made always taste best.

1/2 cup grapeseed or vegetable oil

12 scallions, root ends trimmed, white and green parts chopped thinly or coarsely

1   In a small saucepan, heat the oil over medium heat, and stir-fry the scallions, stirring occasionally until light golden on the edges, about 3 minutes. Turn off the heat and let cool completely before transferring both scallions and oil to a glass jar.

Calories 85	Sodium 0 mg
Calories from Fat 80	Potassium 60 mg
Total Fat 9.0 g	Total Carbohydrate 2 g
Saturated Fat 0.9 g	Dietary Fiber 1 g
Trans Fat 0.0 g	Sugars 1 g
Cholesterol 0 mg	Protein 0 g

EXCHANGES/ CHOICES
2 Fat

PICKLED DAIKON, CABBAGE, CUCUMBER, AND CARROTS

SERVES 16 | SERVING SIZE: 1/4 CUP

A combination of pickled daikon, cabbage, cucumber, and carrot is often served in Chinese restaurants to whet the appetite. These are slightly sweet, savory, and tangy. Rice vinegar is used here because it is milder than the average white vinegar, which tends to be harsh. When choosing rice vinegar, be sure to buy plain vinegar not labeled "seasoned." These pickles keep for months refrigerated, but the longer the vegetables sit in the pickling liquid, the softer they get.

1 small cucumber, quartered lengthwise, seeded, and cut into 2-inch-long pieces

1 large carrot, peeled and cut into matchsticks

1/4 small daikon, peeled and cut into thin rounds, or 8 small white radishes, halved or quartered

1/8 small green cabbage, cut into 1/2-inch strips (about 1 1/2 cups)

1 tablespoon low-sodium salt

1 1/4 cup rice vinegar

1/4 cup agave nectar

1 Set a larger colander over a mixing bowl, and add the cucumber, carrots, daikon, and cabbage. Sprinkle with salt, toss, and let drain for 1 hour. Squeeze the vegetables to release any excess water before transferring them to a quart jar or similar container.

2 In a small mixing bowl, whisk together the vinegar and agave nectar until fully combined. Pour over the vegetables. Close jar with lid and refrigerate.

Calories 35	Sodium 375 mg
Calories from Fat 0	Potassium 70 mg
Total Fat 0.0 g	Total Carbohydrate 8 g
Saturated Fat 0.0 g	Dietary Fiber 0 g
Trans Fat 0.0 g	Sugars 7 g
Cholesterol 0 mg	Protein 0 g

EXCHANGES/ CHOICES
1/2 Carbohydrate

PICKLED CURRY-GARLIC JAPANESE CUCUMBERS

SERVES 10 | SERVING SIZE: 3 PIECES

Pickles are easy to make and are a quick and healthy snack before any meal or as a side dish to help digest meat or seafood entrées. The pickling liquid is a basic three-part concoction of rice vinegar, agave nectar or local honey, and salt, which can be enhanced with refreshing herbs, such as dill, mint, or cilantro, and spices like curry powder or cayenne pepper.

- 8 Persian or Japanese cucumbers, halved lengthwise
- 1 tablespoon low-sodium salt
- 8 medium garlic cloves, peeled and lightly crushed
- 2 red Thai chilies, halved, stems and seeds removed
- 2 cups rice vinegar
- 2 tablespoons agave nectar or local honey
- 2 teaspoons Indian curry powder

1 In a colander set over a bowl, add the cucumbers and sprinkle them with salt. Let drain for 1 hour, wipe each piece clean, and transfer to a glass quart jar. Add the garlic and chilies.

2 Meanwhile in a bowl, whisk together the vinegar, agave nectar, and curry powder. Pour mixture over cucumbers. Secure with lid, and store in a dark cool place, or refrigerate, for at least 48 hours before serving. These can last weeks.

		EXCHANGES/CHOICES
Calories 35	Sodium 120 mg	1 Vegetable
Calories from Fat 0	Potassium 410 mg	
Total Fat 0.0 g	Total Carbohydrate 8 g	
Saturated Fat 0.0 g	Dietary Fiber 1 g	
Trans Fat 0.0 g	Sugars 5 g	
Cholesterol 0 mg	Protein 1 g	

CHAPTER TWO
Soups

Soups are at the core of most meals in Asia. Asian chicken stock flavored with ginger and scallions can be served in a cup as a side for sipping throughout the meal. In Asia, a cup of broth often replaces the beverage, while tea is served at the end of the meal to help digest it. One of the most popular Asian soups enjoyed in the U.S. is Japanese miso soup. In its simplest version, miso soup is made with miso (soybean) paste, kelp stock, wakame seaweed, tofu, and scallions. To make it heartier, you can always add mushrooms. You can spice it up with freshly julienned ginger and some sliced scallions.

Many other types of soups exist throughout Asia. Some are noodle-based; others are rice-based. Generally, noodle-based soups are clear. The noodles are boiled in water, drained, and transferred to a large bowl, then topped with a generous ladle of hot broth. Meat, seafood, vegetables, and herbs are added to the broth just before serving.

Rice soups are also known as *congee* and are similar in texture to hot oatmeal. These porridges, along with noodle soups, are considered comfort food in Asia and are often served when feeling under the weather. However, they are delicious any time of the day and appropriate for any season, though they do warm the heart during the coldest months of the year.

All types of rice grains can be used for making congees. Congees can be plain and served with toppings or sides, or they can be cooked with ingredients and served as flavored congees. Depending on the country of origin, congees can be made with jasmine rice or sushi rice. That said, sushi rice—a medium grain rice—is an ideal choice for making congee as it has a slighty sticky texture and makes a nice thick porridge. Top your bowl of congee with sliced leftover chicken and stir-fried vegetables, some fresh cilantro, a squirt or two of soy sauce and a light drizzle of dark sesame oil, and you have yourself a quick, tasty meal that can be enjoyed for breakfast, lunch, or dinner!

SPICY COCONUT BEAN SOUP

SERVES 12 | SERVING SIZE: 1/2 CUP

This creamy coconut milk and bean soup is spiced with red Thai curry paste. Not too thick and not too thin, this delicious soup will warm your heart and may quickly become one of your favorite comfort foods.

1 tablespoon grapeseed oil

2 tablespoons red Thai curry paste

1 tablespoon coconut palm sugar or agave nectar

1 1/2 tablespoons fish sauce

2 cups light unsweetened coconut milk

1 1/2 quarts unsalted or low-sodium vegetable stock

2 cups chopped string beans

3 medium carrots, peeled and chopped

4 cups cooked navy beans

Juice of 2 limes (about 1/3 cup)

Freshly ground black pepper

1 cup cilantro leaves

1 In a large stockpot over medium heat, add the oil and fry the curry paste until it turns a shade darker, about 1 minute. Add the palm sugar and stir for 1 minute. Add the fish sauce, coconut milk, stock, string beans, carrots, and navy beans.

2 Bring to a boil over high heat. Reduce heat to a simmer and cook, partially covered and stirring occasionally, until the navy beans have broken down, 30 to 45 minutes. Add the lime juice and season with pepper to taste.

3 Serve the soup in individual soup bowls and garnish with cilantro leaves.

		EXCHANGES/ CHOICES
Calories 155	Sodium 355 mg	1 Starch
Calories from Fat 35	Potassium 465 mg	1 Vegetable
Total Fat 4.0 g	Total Carbohydrate 24 g	1 Fat
Saturated Fat 2.2 g	Dietary Fiber 8 g	
Trans Fat 0.0 g	Sugars 4 g	
Cholesterol 0 mg	Protein 7 g	

VELVETY CRAB AND ASPARAGUS SOUP

SERVES 6 | SERVING SIZE: 1 CUP

This crab and asparagus soup has been a Vietnamese classic since French Colonial times. Asparagus is a vegetable the French could not grow in Vietnam. Craving their velouté d'asperges (creamy asparagus soup), they imported the canned vegetable directly from France in the hopes of recreating the classic French soup. Vietnamese cooks, however, reinterpreted the soup and gave it a chunky texture and unique flavor by replacing the cream with crabmeat. The results are absolutely delicious.

8 cups Asian chicken stock (page 17)

1 1/2 cups cooked lump crabmeat

3 cups steamed or boiled green asparagus, drained and coarsely chopped

Freshly ground black pepper

2 egg whites, lightly beaten

1 1/2 tablespoons tapioca starch or cornstarch

6 large sprigs cilantro, leaves only

Fried Garlic Oil (page 19)

1 Bring the stock to a boil in a medium saucepan over high heat. Reduce heat to medium-low, add the crabmeat and asparagus, and adjust seasoning to taste with pepper. Partially cover and let simmer, allowing the flavors to mingle, about 15 minutes.

2 In a steady stream, gently stir in the egg whites, and let the soup simmer until they are fully cooked, about 1 minute. Mix the tapioca starch with 3 tablespoons water thoroughly, and stir into the soup continuously until well distributed and the soup thickens slightly, about 1 minute more.

3 Serve in individual soup bowls garnished with cilantro and some fried garlic oil to taste.

Calories 70	Sodium 320 mg	**EXCHANGES/ CHOICES**
Calories from Fat 10	Potassium 345 mg	1 Vegetable
Total Fat 1.0 g	Total Carbohydrate 6 g	1 Lean Meat
Saturated Fat 0.2 g	Dietary Fiber 2 g	
Trans Fat 0.0 g	Sugars 1 g	
Cholesterol 35 mg	Protein 11 g	

ASIAN-STYLE SPLIT PEA SOUP

SERVES 9 | SERVING SIZE: 1 CUP

This recipe is a new take on the classic American split pea soup and a favorite comfort food for many. Here the chicken or vegetable stock is made fragrant with curry powder and rendered slightly spicy with cayenne pepper.

1 tablespoon grapeseed or vegetable oil

4 large garlic cloves, crushed, peeled, and chopped

1 ounce (1 1/2-inch piece) ginger, peeled and finely grated

1 small onion, peeled and minced

1 tablespoon Indian curry powder

1/2 teaspoon cayenne powder (optional)

2 1/2 quarts Asian Chicken Stock (page 17)

3 large carrots, peeled and chopped

2 cups dried green peas

Freshly ground black pepper

1. In a large pot over medium heat, add the oil and sauté the garlic, ginger, and onion until golden, about 10 minutes. Add the curry powder and continue to stir-fry for 1 minute. Add the cayenne, stock, carrots, and green peas, and bring to a boil.

2. Reduce heat to low, and cook until the peas break down and thicken the soup, making it almost smooth in consistency, about 3 to 4 hours. Season with pepper to taste and serve hot.

Calories 185	Sodium 160 mg
Calories from Fat 20	Potassium 575 mg
Total Fat 2.5 g	Total Carbohydrate 30 g
Saturated Fat 0.4 g	Dietary Fiber 11 g
Trans Fat 0.0 g	Sugars 5 g
Cholesterol 5 mg	Protein 12 g

EXCHANGES/CHOICES
1 1/2 Starch
1 Lean Meat
1/2 Fat

SWEET POTATO AND GINGER SOUP

SERVES 6 | **SERVING SIZE: 1 CUP**

Sweet potatoes are full of nutrients, and ginger is a cure-all. When combined, these two delicious ingredients make a healthy cocktail that can be served chilled, at room temperature, or hot, depending on the season. The freshly grated ginger juice lightens this sweet soup with just enough spice.

3 large sweet potatoes, peeled and diced (8 ounces each)

3 cups filtered water

2 ounces ginger, grated and juiced (about 2 tablespoons)

1 teaspoon low-sodium salt

1 In a medium pot over medium heat, add the sweet potatoes, water, ginger juice, and salt. Cook until sweet potatoes are tender.

2 Working in batches, transfer potatoes and cooking water to a blender or food processor and process to a smooth consistency.

Calories 85
  Calories from Fat 0
Total Fat 0.0 g
  Saturated Fat 0.0 g
  Trans Fat 0.0 g
  Cholesterol 0 mg

Sodium 165 mg
Potassium 265 mg
Total Carbohydrate 19 g
  Dietary Fiber 3 g
  Sugars 6 g
  Protein 2 g

EXCHANGES/ CHOICES
1 Starch

COCONUT CURRY RICE NOODLE SOUP WITH CHICKEN

SERVES 6 | SERVING SIZE: 2 1/2 CUPS

Inspired by the famous northern Thai curry noodle soup known as kao soi, this soup is perfect for any time of the year. In Asia, soup is eaten every day. For a different but equally delicious version, substitute tiger shrimp for the chicken. You can make several different versions of this soup by adding tiger shrimp in place of chicken, or bok choy, shitake mushrooms, and cubed tofu, for a vegetarian version. Feel free to experiment.

2 tablespoons grapeseed or vegetable oil

2 large garlic cloves, crushed, peeled, and finely chopped

1 large shallot, peeled and finely chopped

1 tablespoon Thai red curry paste

1 tablespoon Indian curry powder

6 1/2 cups Asian Chicken Stock (page 17)

1 1/2 cups light unsweetened coconut milk

1 1/2 tablespoons agave nectar or pure maple syrup

Juice of 1 lemon (about 1/3 cup)

12 ounces rice sticks, softened in cold water until pliable

12 ounces chicken breast, thinly sliced, or 24 small headless tiger shrimp, peeled and deveined

18 Thai basil leaves or 12 sprigs cilantro, leaves only

1   In a medium saucepan over medium-high heat, add the oil and stir-fry the garlic and shallot until golden, about 2 minutes. Add the curry paste and powder, and toast until fragrant and one shade darker, about 30 seconds. Stir in the stock, coconut milk, agave nectar, and lemon juice and bring to a boil. Reduce heat to low and cover.

2   Meanwhile, bring a medium pot of water to a boil, and cook the rice noodles until tender yet firm, about 30 seconds. Drain completely and divide among 6 large soup bowls.

3   Add the chicken to the soup stock, and cook until opaque, about 1 minute. Bring to a boil, and turn off the heat. Ladle a generous amount of broth over each serving of noodles, along with chicken. Garnish each individual serving with basil or cilantro before serving.

		EXCHANGES/ CHOICES
Calories 395	Sodium 385 mg	3 Starch
Calories from Fat 90	Potassium 350 mg	1/2 Carbohydrate
Total Fat 0.0 g	Total Carbohydrate 56 g	2 Lean Meat
Saturated Fat 4.1 g	Dietary Fiber 2 g	1 Fat
Trans Fat 0.0 g	Sugars 5 g	
Cholesterol 35 mg	Protein 18 g	

TANGY RICE NOODLE SOUP WITH PORK AND SHRIMP

SERVES 6 | SERVING SIZE: 2 1/2 CUPS

Kway'teo is another popular rice noodle soup. This version with ground pork and shrimp is easy to prepare, and the broth can be served over the noodles or on the side for sipping—as is common practice in some parts of Southeast Asia. Either way, this soup is delicious.

8 cups Asian Pork Stock (variation, page 17)

12 ounces coarsely ground pork

12 ounces rice sticks, softened in cold water until pliable

18 small, headless tiger shrimp, peeled, deveined, and halved lengthwise

2 cups mung bean sprouts, blanched

3 scallions, trimmed and thinly sliced

1 cup cilantro leaves

Fried Garlic Oil (page 19)

1 lemon or lime, sliced into 6 equal wedges

Chili-garlic sauce

Fish sauce

1 In a medium stockpot, bring the stock to a boil over medium-high heat. In small batches, place some ground pork in a ladle, and lower it just enough into the stockpot to allow some of the broth into it. With a fork, stir the pork with the broth until it separates, and release into the broth. Repeat this until all of the pork is added to the broth. Reduce heat to low, and cover for now.

2 Meanwhile, bring a pot of water to a boil, and cook the noodles until tender yet firm, about 30 seconds. Drain and divide among 6 large soup bowls.

3 Add the shrimp to the broth, and cook until opaque, about 30 seconds. Ladle a generous amount of broth along with pork and shrimp to each serving of rice noodles. Garnish with mung bean sprouts, scallions, cilantro, and fried garlic (with some oil if you wish), according to taste. Squeeze a wedge of lemon or lime on top. Add some chili-garlic sauce, and adjust seasoning with fish sauce to taste, if desired.

		EXCHANGES/ CHOICES
Calories 405	Sodium 420 mg	3 1/2 Starch
Calories from Fat 100	Potassium 330 mg	2 Lean Meat
Total Fat 11.0 g	Total Carbohydrate 52 g	1 Fat
Saturated Fat 3.5 g	Dietary Fiber 2 g	
Trans Fat 0.1 g	Sugars 2 g	
Cholesterol 120 mg	Protein 24 g	

GLASS NOODLE SOUP WITH CUCUMBER AND GROUND PORK

SERVES 6 | SERVING SIZE: 2 1/2 CUPS

Glass noodles, also known as cellophane or crystal noodles, are popular in Asia. There are two main types, including a thin one made from mung bean starch (sometimes labeled as "bean thread") and a thicker version that is grayish in color and made from sweet potato starch. Somewhat flavorless, glass noodles have the ability to absorb a great deal of flavor and are enjoyed for their chewy texture. The thin ones are best used in soups or as filler in dumplings or spring rolls, while the thicker ones are best for stir-frying.

8 cups Asian Pork Stock (variation, page 17)

12 ounces coarsely ground pork

8 1/2 ounces Chinese mung bean starch noodles (about 5 individual), soaked in water until pliable

1 small hothouse cucumber, peeled, halved lengthwise, seeded, and cut crosswise into 1/4-inch thick slices

2 cups cilantro leaves

Fried Garlic Oil (page 19)

Fish sauce

1   In a medium stockpot, bring the stock to a boil over medium-high heat. In small batches, place some ground pork in a ladle and lower it just enough into the stockpot to allow some of the broth into it. With a fork, stir the pork with the broth until it separates, and release into the broth. Repeat this until all of the pork is added to the broth. Reduce heat to low, and cover.

2   Meanwhile, bring a pot of water to a boil, and cook the noodles until fully translucent, about 1 minute. Drain and divide among 6 large soup bowls.

3   Add the cucumber to the broth, and cook for 1 minute. Ladle a generous amount of broth with pork and cucumber over each serving of noodles, and garnish with cilantro and fried garlic oil to taste. Adjust seasoning with fish sauce, if desired.

Calories 280	Sodium 215 mg	**EXCHANGES/ CHOICES**
Calories from Fat 90	Potassium 225 mg	2 1/2 Starch
Total Fat 10.0 g	Total Carbohydrate 36 g	1 Lean Meat
Saturated Fat 3.2 g	Dietary Fiber 1 g	1 Fat
Trans Fat 0.1 g	Sugars 0 g	
Cholesterol 45 mg	Protein 12 g	

SOBA NOODLES WITH VEGETABLES IN SEAWEED BROTH

SERVES 6 | SERVING SIZE: 2 1/2 CUPS

A noodle made of wheat and buckwheat flour, soba is a specialty of northern Japan. A healthy alternative to plain wheat flour noodles or Italian pasta, soba is often served cold. Kelp seaweed gives the dish a unique flavor, balancing an otherwise sweet and savory vegetarian broth.

5 cups spring or filtered water

1 large piece (2 × 4-inch piece) of kombu (kelp)

12 medium dried shitake mushrooms, soaked in at least 3 cups of water until pliable (soaking water filtered and reserved)

2 tablespoons light soy sauce

1 cup sake

1 tablespoon agave nectar

1 large carrot, peeled and sliced thinly

3 cups broccoli florets

6 individual bundles soba or green tea soba noodles, paper rings removed

2-inch piece ginger, peeled, and thinly julienned (thread-like)

Fried Scallion Oil (page 20)

1 Pour the water in a medium-sized stockpot, add the kelp, and bring to a boil over high heat. Reduce heat to low, and simmer for 30 minutes.

2 Meanwhile, drain the shitakes, reserving 3 cups of the soaking liquid. Remove stems from mushrooms, and halve the caps. Strain the mushroom liquid through a paper-towel-lined sieve, and transfer the liquid and caps to the stockpot along with soy sauce, sake, and agave nectar. Add the carrots, and continue to simmer until tender, yet firm, about 5 minutes. Add the broccoli and simmer for an additional 5 minutes.

3 Bring a separate pot of water to a boil, and cook the soba until tender, yet firm, about 2 minutes. Drain, shock under cold running water, and drain again. Divide noodles among 6 large individual soup bowls. Ladle a generous amount of broth along with mushrooms, carrots, and broccoli florets. Garnish with ginger and Fried Scallion Oil (page 20), if desired.

Calories 180	**Sodium** 405 mg
Calories from Fat 0	**Potassium** 365 mg
Total Fat 0.0 g	**Total Carbohydrate** 36 g
Saturated Fat 0.1 g	**Dietary Fiber** 4 g
Trans Fat 0.0 g	**Sugars** 7 g
Cholesterol 0 mg	**Protein** 7 g

EXCHANGES/ CHOICES
1 1/2 Starch
1/2 Carbohydrate
1 Vegetable

MISO SOUP WITH SILKEN TOFU, WAKAME, AND MUSHROOMS

SERVES 6 | **SERVING SIZE: 1 1/2 CUPS**

A classic Japanese starter, miso soup is very simple to make, and you can add other ingredients to this basic version with tofu, mushrooms, and seaweed. For example, small clams or mussels would make for a delicious seafood version.

1 1/2 quarts filtered or spring water

2 6-inch pieces kombu (kelp seaweed)

1/4 cup white miso (shiro-miso)

1/2 cup sake

1/3 cup dried wakame seaweed, soaked until soft, then drained and chopped

1 pound silken tofu, drained and cubed

2 scallions, trimmed and chopped

2 ounces fresh ginger, peeled and very finely julienned (thread-like)

4 ounces enoki mushrooms

Toasted sesame seeds

1 Add the water and kombu to a medium-size pot, and bring to a boil over high heat. Reduce heat to low and stir in the miso and sake and simmer for 15 minutes. Add the wakame and tofu and cook for 1 minute.

2 Divide among individual soup bowls, and garnish with scallions, ginger, enoki, mushrooms, and toasted sesame seeds.

Calories 95	**Sodium** 290 mg
Calories from Fat 20	**Potassium** 280 mg
Total Fat 2.5 g	**Total Carbohydrate** 10 g
Saturated Fat 0.3 g	**Dietary Fiber** 1 g
Trans Fat 0.0 g	**Sugars** 4 g
Cholesterol 0 mg	**Protein** 7 g

EXCHANGES/ CHOICES
1/2 Carbohydrate
1 Lean Meat
1/2 Fat

SPICY AND SOUR SHRIMP SOUP

SERVES 6 | SERVING SIZE: 1 1/2 CUPS

This classic Thai shrimp soup makes for a great starter or can be served as a light lunch with rice on the side. Like any other Southeast Asian sour soup, this one will refresh your palate and quench your thirst. Key ingredients such as lemongrass, kaffir lime leaves, galangal, and tamarind may be hard to find outside of an Asian market. Make the effort to find them, though, as the resulting dish is sublime.

10 cups Asian Chicken Stock (page 17)

3 stalks lemongrass, outer leaves and dry green tops discarded, bulb and stalk lightly crushed

2-inch piece galangal (fresh, frozen, or dried), sliced

6 fresh, frozen, or dried kaffir lime leaves

1 1/2 tablespoons fish sauce

1/4 cup tamarind, or juice of 1 lime

3 dried chilies

24 small to medium headless tiger shrimp, shelled and deveined

1 medium ripe tomato, cut into 8 wedges

1 cup canned straw mushrooms, rinsed and drained, or 6 fresh small to medium shitakes, stems removed and caps quartered

2 scallions, trimmed and cut into 1-inch pieces

4 sprigs fresh Thai basil, about 1/3 cup leaves, or 1/3 cup fresh cilantro leaves

Fried Garlic Oil (page 19)

1 In a medium stockpot, bring the stock to a boil over medium-high heat, and reduce heat to medium-low. Add the lemongrass, galangal, kaffir lime leaves, fish sauce, and chilies, and simmer until reduced by 2 cups, about 1 hour. Add the shrimp, tomatoes, mushrooms, and scallions, and cook until the shrimp turn opaque, about 2 minutes.

2 Serve in individual soup bowls, garnished with basil or cilantro and Fried Garlic Oil (page 19) as desired.

Calories 105
  Calories from Fat 15
Total Fat 1.5 g
  Saturated Fat 0.4 g
  Trans Fat 0.0 g
Cholesterol 110 mg

Sodium 705 mg
Potassium 295 mg
Total Carbohydrate 8 g
  Dietary Fiber 1 g
  Sugars 2 g
Protein 14 g

EXCHANGES/ CHOICES
1 Vegetable
2 Lean Meat

SOUR PINEAPPLE, TOMATO, AND FISH SOUP WITH FRIED GARLIC

SERVES 6 | **SERVING SIZE: 1 1/2 CUPS**

"Sour soups" as they are often called, are popular in Southeast Asia, and generally include seafood and a souring ingredient, most often lime or tamarind, and sometimes star fruit, also known as "carambola." They are savory, refreshing, and often spicy as well. Complete with fresh pineapple and tomato, this soup is perfect served any time of the year, even on a hot summer day. After all, in tropical Asia, piping hot soups are eaten every day.

8 cups Asian Chicken Stock (page 17)

1/4 small fresh pineapple, peeled and cut into bite-size chunks

2 medium-ripe red tomatoes, each cut into 8 thick wedges

3 dried whole red chilies

Juice of 1 lime (about 1/4 cup)

1 pound cod steaks or filets, cut into 2-inch pieces

Low-sodium salt

Freshly ground black pepper

1/3 cup tightly packed cilantro leaves (about 12 to 15 sprigs)

Fried Garlic Oil (page 19)

1 In a medium stockpot, bring the stock to a boil over medium-high heat, and reduce heat to medium-low. Add the pineapple, tomatoes, chilies, lime juice, and fish.

2 Adjust seasoning with salt and pepper, reduce heat to low, and continue to simmer until the flavors blend, about 15 minutes.

3 Serve, garnished with cilantro and Fried Garlic Oil (page 19), as desired.

Calories 90	Sodium 365 mg
Calories from Fat 10	Potassium 470 mg
Total Fat 1.0 g	Total Carbohydrate 4 g
Saturated Fat 0.1 g	Dietary Fiber 1 g
Trans Fat 0.0 g	Sugars 3 g
Cholesterol 40 mg	Protein 16 g

EXCHANGES/ CHOICES
2 Lean Meat

SWEET AND SPICY LENTIL SOUP

SERVES 6 | SERVING SIZE: 1 CUP

Lentils are eaten throughout India, oftentimes served commonly as dips called "dal." This soup is inspired by these dips, extended with unsweetened rice milk, and mildly spiced with Indian curry powder. The caramelized shallots and red pepper add the sweetness and color to this velvety red lentil soup.

2 tablespoons grapeseed or vegetable oil

1 small onion, peeled and minced

4 garlic cloves, peeled and minced

2 ounces ginger, peeled and minced

1 1/2 tablespoons Indian curry powder

1 1/2 cup light unsweetened coconut milk

2 1/2 cups unsweetened rice milk

4 cups water

Juice of 1 lemon (about 1/4 cup)

1 tablespoon agave nectar

2 cups dried red lentils

1 bunch cilantro, leaves only (1 cup tightly packed leaves)

1 In a medium stockpot, add the oil and sauté the onion, garlic, and ginger over medium heat until golden, about 5 minutes. Stir in the curry until one shade darker, about 30 seconds. Add the coconut and rice milks, 4 cups water, lemon juice, agave nectar, and dried lentils.

2 Cook, covered, until the lentils have absorbed liquid, broken down and thickened the soup, about 2 hours.

3 Stir in the cilantro, and serve in individual soup bowls.

		EXCHANGES/ CHOICES
Calories 360	**Sodium** 50 mg	2 1/2 Starch
Calories from Fat 90	**Potassium** 945 mg	1/2 Carbohydrate
Total Fat 10.0 g	**Total Carbohydrate** 53 g	2 Lean Meat
Saturated Fat 3.7 g	**Dietary Fiber** 15 g	1 Fat
Trans Fat 0.0 g	**Sugars** 13 g	
Cholesterol 0 mg	**Protein** 19 g	

BROWN RICE CONGEE WITH STIR-FRIED HERBS

SERVES 6 | SERVING SIZE: 1 CUP

Congee, or rice porridge, is eaten throughout Asia. It is a great way to make a small amount of rice go a long way. Adorned with stir-fried ginger, scallion, cilantro, and chilies, this congee is a step up from the plain version and still perfect for pairing with all sorts of meat, seafood, or vegetable sides. Sushi rice is particularly wonderful for making porridge because the grain is semi-sticky, rendering a texture that thickens easily and holds together.

2 quarts filtered water

1 cup brown sushi rice

1 tablespoon grapeseed or vegetable oil

2 ounces ginger, peeled and finely julienned

2 scallions, trimmed and julienned into 1-inch-long pieces

2 red Thai chilies, stems and seeds removed, thinly sliced into rounds

1/2 bunch cilantro, stems trimmed and coarsely chopped (about 1 cup)

1 Fill a large pot with the water. Add the rice, cover, and bring to a boil over high heat. Reduce heat to medium, and continue to cook until the rice grains break down and the soup thickens, about 1 hour.

2 Meanwhile in a small skillet over high heat, add the oil and stir-fry the ginger, scallions, and chilies until fragrant and lightly golden, 30 to 45 seconds. Add the cilantro and continue to stir-fry until just wilted, about 30 seconds more. Transfer to a bowl.

3 Ladle some congee into 6 individual bowls, and top each with about 1 tablespoon of stir-fried herbs. Mix the herbs into the porridge to distribute the flavors. Serve.

Calories 150	Sodium 20 mg	**EXCHANGES/ CHOICES**
Calories from Fat 30	Potassium 170 mg	2 Starch
Total Fat 3.5 g	Total Carbohydrate 27 g	
Saturated Fat 0.4 g	Dietary Fiber 2 g	
Trans Fat 0.0 g	Sugars 1 g	
Cholesterol 0 mg	Protein 3 g	

SPICY BROWN RICE CONGEE WITH CHICKEN AND LEMONGRASS

SERVES 6 | **SERVING SIZE: 1 CUP**

This Congee is Vietnamese-inspired and made using long-grain jasmine brown rice. Flavored with lemongrass and red Thai chilies, every spoonful is refreshing, especially with a hint of freshly torn Thai basil or cilantro. This chicken rice soup is perfect for warming up the body during those cold winter nights.

1 1/2 cups brown jasmine rice

2 quarts Basic Asian Chicken Stock (page 17)

2 stalks lemongrass, outer leaves, root end, and tough dry tops trimmed, 8-inch bulb lightly crushed

8 ounces boneless, skinless chicken breasts or thighs, thinly sliced

1 or 2 red Thai chilies, stems and seeds removed, thinly sliced

12 sprigs cilantro, coarsely chopped, or 12 Thai basil leaves, freshly torn

1 Fill a large pot with the rice, stock, and lemongrass cover and bring to a boil over high heat. Reduce heat to medium, and continue to cook until the rice grains break down and the soup thickens, about 1 hour.

2 Add the chicken and chili, and continue to simmer until the chicken is cooked through, about 15 minutes more.

3 Serve garnished with cilantro or Thai basil.

Calories 230	Sodium 190 mg
Calories from Fat 20	Potassium 200 mg
Total Fat 2.5 g	Total Carbohydrate 36 g
Saturated Fat 0.6 g	Dietary Fiber 2 g
Trans Fat 0.0 g	Sugars 1 g
Cholesterol 25 mg	Protein 14 g

EXCHANGES/ CHOICES
2 1/2 Starch
1 Lean Meat

CHAPTER THREE
Finger Foods

In China, finger foods are generally referred to as "dim sum," which can be roughly translated as "touch of the heart." This seems appropriate for describing bite-sized morsels. Other parts of Asia offer finger foods as well, mostly in the form of dumplings, spring rolls, and skewered foods popularly known to as "satay."

This chapter is devoted to foods that can easily be served as appetizers hors-d'oeuvres for a cocktail party or simply for creating small tasting plates to share with friends and family. Finger foods can take time to make, but they also make for a great excuse to socialize. In Asia, finger foods such as spring rolls and dumplings are often made in large quantities, requiring a few friends or members of the family, generally women, to get together, share stories, sip tea, and make hundreds of small, beautifully shaped morsels. At home, you can do the same and invite friends to help you create finger foods. This way, what may seem a tedious task at first glance will not be so overwhelming in the end.

Accompanied by dipping sauces, the fillings are generally lightly seasoned if at all. Finger foods are also all about the technique. Once you've learned how to shape them, the possibilities for fillings are endless. You can fill dumpling or spring roll wrappers with all sorts of fillings, like ground meat, chopped seafood, or vegetables, seasoning any of these lightly with soy sauce or dark sesame oil, and throwing some freshly minced ginger and scallion in the mix. You can also fill them with fruit and serve as a sweet snack with tea in the afternoon.

Finger foods are also ideal for creating balanced meals that are proportioned. And, because they are easy to pack, they're perfect for lunch at the office or school.

MAKING DUMPLINGS AHEAD TO SAVE TIME

Most finger foods can be made ahead of time, saving you a great deal of time during the week when you are tired and only have a few minutes to get dinner on the table.

For example, dumplings can be shaped and placed on a plate in a single layer, without touching one another. Place them in the freezer, and when they are rock hard, transfer them to a sealable plastic bag. Leave them in the freezer, and only take out a handful at a time for dinner.

Boil, steam, or pan-fry dumplings, and serve them simply with soy sauce and hot sauce on the side for dipping for a quick and hearty meal.

COOKING VARIATIONS FOR DUMPLINGS

BOILING: Bring a large pot of water to a boil, and cook until the dumplings float to the top. Then time 1 minute and drain before serving.

STEAMING: Simply place a bamboo steamer over a wok filled with water. Line the bamboo steamer with a lettuce leaf, and place the dumplings on top, about 1 inch apart. Place the lid on top and cook through, about 5 minutes total.

PAN-FRYING: In a large nonstick skillet, add 3 tablespoons grapeseed oil and 3 tablespoons water. Add the dumplings, cover with a lid, and bring to a boil over medium-high heat. Cook until the water evaporates completely and the oil is left behind and starts crisping the underside of the dumpling. Remove the pot-stickers from

the pan, drain on paper towel, and serve hot. For every batch, replenish the water. Replenish with oil every other batch, replenish with 3 tablespoons water, and 1 tablespoon oil.

When making pot-stickers, you are steaming and frying simultaneously. The dumplings in this technique are never flipped, so that the underside is golden crisp while the top-side appears steamed.

MAKING SPRING ROLLS AHEAD TO SAVE TIME

Spring rolls can be served fresh (uncooked) or baked using less oil than the popular deep-fried versions. The filling options are endless.

SUMMER ROLLS USING RICE PAPER

Summer rolls (aka "fresh summer rolls") using rice paper can be made up to two hours ahead of time but should not be refrigerated, or the rice paper will harden and become unpleasantly chewy.

When using rice papers, be sure to soak them in water one at a time for a couple of minutes to soften. Then, transfer them to a clean wood surface, and blot them dry with a paper towel, removing any excess water and rendering the paper sticky rather than slippery. Sticky paper is ideal for rolling and holding the filling in place.

Place the filling in the side closest to you, then lift that side up and fold it over the filling. Fold in the sides, and roll tightly—being careful not to tear the paper—to the end. This technique is used whether you are making fresh or cooked spring rolls. Like dumplings, it's all in the technique. Once you know how to shape summer rolls, the fillings are endless.

Summer rolls are the best option if you're watching your calories. Base ingredients in the summer rolls are generally raw, including fresh lettuce, shredded carrots, julienned cucumber, and fresh herbs such as mint, cilantro, or Thai basil.

Protein can include leftover shredded meats, such as pork, chicken, or beef. Poached seafood, such as shrimp, crabmeat, or lobster, will do as well. Tofu is a great vegetarian protein and can be used straight from the package. Drain, cut into 1/2-inch sticks, and add to the spring roll as is or pan-fried until golden for added texture.

BAKED SPRING ROLLS USING WHEAT WRAPPERS

The technique for making spring rolls is the same as for rice paper (see reference to "summer rolls" above), except that soaking each wrapper in water is not necessary. These store-bought refrigerated or frozen wrappers are pliable and ready to work with.

Place the filling on the side closest to you, lifting the bottom pointy side up and folding it over the filling once. Then fold in the sides and continue rolling, brushing halfway through with egg wash to seal the roll.

You can use store-bought refrigerated or frozen wheat wrappers to make spring rolls ahead of time. Fill them with any number of chopped raw proteins and vegetable fillings, or fruit fillings

to serve as dessert. Once rolled, place them on a cookie sheet, a half-inch apart. Place them in the freezer until rock solid, then transfer them in a sealable plastic bag and return them to the freezer.

Brush the spring rolls lightly with vegetable oil, and bake at 375°F until golden all around, about 15–20 minutes. Though not as crispy as the deep-fried version, baked spring rolls are tasty and guilt-free.

CURRY POTATO AND SWEET PEA SAMOSAS

SERVES 12 | SERVING SIZE: 1 PIECE

This baked spring roll is a healthy alternative to the classic deep-fried version. Baked flaky samosas are a type of fried dumpling. An Indian specialty, they are a perfect finger food that can be served at a cocktail party or as an appetizer. While puff pastry is often used, here, fresh eggroll wrappers are used to reduce the fat content.

2 flaky potatoes (8 ounces each), baked and crushed until smooth

1 cup cooked green peas, crushed until smooth

1 large garlic clove, peeled and grated

1 ounce ginger, peeled and grated

2 teaspoons Indian curry powder

Low-sodium salt

Freshly ground black pepper

12 square fresh eggroll wrappers

2 tablespoons grapeseed oil for brushing

1 Preheat the oven to 375°F for 20 minutes.

2 Meanwhile, in a bowl, mix together the potatoes, peas, garlic, ginger, and curry powder. Season to taste with salt and pepper, and continue to mix until well combined.

3 Take one square eggroll wrapper, and fill with 2 tablespoons of filling. Wet the inside corners and sides of the wrapper by dabbing lightly with water. Gather opposite corners toward the center, pinching the sides together to form a 4-sided pyramid. Repeat with remaining ingredients until you have 12 samosas. Brush lightly with oil, and bake until golden, 10 to 15 minutes.

Calories 150	**Sodium** 185 mg
Calories from Fat 25	**Potassium** 180 mg
Total Fat 3.0 g	**Total Carbohydrate** 27 g
Saturated Fat 0.3 g	**Dietary Fiber** 2 g
Trans Fat 0.0 g	**Sugars** 2 g
Cholesterol 5 mg	**Protein** 4 g

EXCHANGES/ CHOICES
2 Starch

SHRIMP AND CABBAGE POT STICKERS

SERVES 48 | SERVING SIZE: 1 POT STICKER

Easy to make at home, pot stickers are steamed and pan-fried simultaneously. These shrimp and cabbage pot stickers are definitely worth the effort, seasoned with a hint of soy sauce and sesame oil, the richness balanced with a vinegar-based dipping sauce. Serve them as hors d'oeuvres for a party, appetizers at dinnertime, or as a one-dish meal.

1/4 small napa cabbage, minced (about 3 cups)

1 pound headless peeled and deveined raw shrimp, minced

1 scallion, trimmed and minced

1-inch piece ginger, peeled and minced

1 tablespoon dark sesame oil

1 1/2 tablespoons light soy sauce

Freshly cracked black pepper

48 fresh round dumpling wrappers

1/2 cup vegetable oil (or see variation)

Water

Herbal Soy Sauce Dressing (page 11)

1 In a large mixing bowl, mix together the cabbage, shrimp, scallion, ginger, sesame oil, soy sauce, and pepper to taste until well combined.

2 Fill a small bowl with water. Start filling your wrappers by placing 1 heaping teaspoon of the cabbage and shrimp filling into the wrapper. Dip your finger in the water, and moisten the inside edge of the dumpling wrapper. Fold the dumpling into a half-moon shape, enclosing the filling and squeezing any air out while sealing the edges in the process. Repeat with the remaining wrappers and filling.

3 In a nonstick pan over medium-high heat, stir in 2 tablespoons vegetable oil and 3 tablespoons water. Place 8 dumplings in a single layer, overlapping if desired. Cover and cook until the water is fully evaporated and the bottoms of the dumplings are golden brown, about 5 minutes. Remove from heat, and transfer the dumplings to a paper-lined plate to drain excess oil before serving.

4 Repeat with remaining dumplings, adding only 1 tablespoon oil and 3 tablespoons water with each batch of 8 dumplings. Serve with Herbal Soy Sauce Dressing (page 11) as a side dip.

VARIATION

Steam for 5 minutes, or boil for 3 minutes and drain.

Calories 50
  Calories from Fat 20
Total Fat 2.5 g
  Saturated Fat 0.2 g
  Trans Fat 0.0 g
Cholesterol 15 mg

Sodium 65 mg
Potassium 40 mg
Total Carbohydrate 4 g
  Dietary Fiber 0 g
  Sugars 0 g
Protein 3 g

EXCHANGES/ CHOICES
1/2 Carbohydrate
1/2 Fat

TOFU POT STICKERS

SERVES 48 | SERVING SIZE: 1 POT STICKER

Tofu pot stickers are wholesome and light and will quickly become a favorite. Tofu has a delicious earthy flavor but also absorbs a great deal of flavor. Here the tofu is mixed with scallion and ginger and seasoned with dark sesame oil and soy sauce. Simple, yet packed with a lot of flavor. *Tip: Use firm tofu packed in water, not "silken."*

2 pounds firm tofu, drained

1 scallion, trimmed and minced

1-inch piece ginger, peeled and grated

1 tablespoons dark sesame oil

1 1/2 tablespoons light soy sauce

Freshly cracked black pepper

48 fresh round dumpling wrappers

1/2 cup vegetable oil, divided use

Herbal Soy Sauce Dressing (page 11)

1 In a large mixing bowl, mix together the tofu, scallion, ginger, sesame oil, soy sauce, and pepper to taste, until well combined.

2 Fill a small bowl with water. Start filling your wrappers by placing 1 heaping teaspoon of the tofu filling into the wrapper. Dip your finger in the water, and moisten the inside edge of the dumpling wrapper. Fold the dumpling into a half-moon shape, enclosing the filling and squeezing any air out while sealing the edges in the process. Repeat with the remaining wrappers and filling.

3 In a nonstick pan over medium-high heat, stir in 2 tablespoons vegetable oil and 3 tablespoons water. Place 8 dumplings in a single layer, overlapping if desired. Cover and cook until the water is fully evaporated and the bottoms of the dumplings are golden brown, about 5 minutes. Remove from heat, and transfer the dumplings to a paper-lined plate to drain excess oil before serving.

4 Repeat with remaining dumplings, adding only 1 tablespoon oil and 3 tablespoons water with each batch of 8 dumplings. Serve with Herbal Soy Sauce Dressing (page 11) as a side dip.

VARIATION

Steam for 5 minutes, or boil for 3 minutes and drain.

		EXCHANGES/CHOICES
Calories 50	Sodium 55 mg	1/2 Carbohydrate
Calories from Fat 25	Potassium 35 mg	1/2 Fat
Total Fat 3.0 g	Total Carbohydrate 4 g	
Saturated Fat 0.4 g	Dietary Fiber 0 g	
Trans Fat 0.0 g	Sugars 0 g	
Cholesterol 0 mg	Protein 2 g	

SHRIMP AND PORK WONTONS

SERVES 48 | SERVING SIZE: 1 POT STICKER

Shrimp and pork are a classic combination in many Asian recipes including wontons, which are a type of dumplings generally served in a light chicken broth. Like many dumplings, they are also delicious simply steamed or boiled and served with a dipping sauce on the side. Feel free to serve them free of broth as finger foods, if you wish, or in broth on a cold winter day.

8 cups Asian Chicken Stock (page 17)

2 tablespoons dark sesame oil, divided use

8 ounces coarsely ground pork (70% lean)

1 pound headless peeled and deveined raw shrimp, minced

1 scallion, trimmed and green and white parts minced

1-inch piece ginger, peeled and grated

1 tablespoon light soy sauce

1 teaspoon tapioca starch or cornstarch

Freshly cracked black pepper

48 fresh square dumpling wrappers

1/2 cup cilantro leaves

1. Pour the chicken stock with 1 tablespoon sesame oil in a medium stockpot, and bring to a boil over medium-high heat. Reduce heat to low and simmer, covered until ready to use.

2. Meanwhile, in a large mixing bowl, mix together the pork, shrimp, scallion, ginger, the remaining sesame oil, soy sauce, tapioca starch, and pepper to taste, until well combined.

3. Fill a small bowl with water. Start filling your wrappers by placing 1 heaping teaspoon of the filling into the wrapper. Dip your finger in the water, and moisten the inside edge of the dumpling wrapper. Fold the dumpling into a half-moon shape, enclosing the filling and squeezing any air out while sealing the edges in the process. Repeat with the remaining wrappers and filling.

4. Bring a medium pot of water to a boil over high heat. Cook the wontons in batches until they float on the surface and are cooked through, about 3 minutes. Divide among 6 large soup bowls. Ladle chicken stock over each serving, and garnish with cilantro as desired before serving.

VARIATION

Steam for 5 minutes, or boil for 3 minutes and drain. Serve with light soy sauce and chili-garlic sauce on the side for dipping, if you wish.

Calories 55	Sodium 100 mg
Calories from Fat 20	Potassium 40 mg
Total Fat 2.0 g	Total Carbohydrate 5 g
Saturated Fat 0.6 g	Dietary Fiber 0 g
Trans Fat 0.0 g	Sugars 0 g
Cholesterol 20 mg	Protein 4 g

EXCHANGES/ CHOICES
1/2 Carbohydrate
1/2 Fat

BAKED VEGETABLE SPRING ROLLS

SERVES 24 | **SERVING SIZE: 1 SPRING ROLL**

Like dumplings, spring rolls can be filled with any combination of meat, seafood, and vegetables. Traditionally, golden crisp spring rolls are deep-fried. These are brushed lightly with oil and baked for a healthier version of the classic. Serve with the Citrus Soy Sauce Dressing (page 14) as a side dip.

2 cups shredded cabbage

1 cup shredded carrot

8 large shitake mushrooms, stems removed and caps julienned

1 tablespoon light soy sauce

1 tablespoon dark sesame oil

Freshly ground black pepper

24 thin Chinese wheat spring roll wrappers

2 eggs, beaten

1/4 cup vegetable oil

Citrus Soy Sauce Dressing (page 14)

1 Preheat the oven to 350°F for 20 minutes.

2 In a mixing bowl, toss together the cabbage, carrots, mushrooms, soy sauce, sesame oil, and pepper to taste, until well combined.

3 Take a wrapper and place it in front of you like a diamond shape. Put 3 tablespoons of cabbage filling at the point closest to you, shaping the filling into a 3-inch log. Fold the point closest to you over the filling, fold in the side points, and roll halfway. Brush egg wash on the end, then proceed with rolling and securing the filling completely. Repeat process with the remaining wrappers and filling.

4 Place the spring rolls in a single layer, on a parchment paper-lined baking sheet. Brush each with oil, and bake until golden and crispy on all sides, 15 to 20 minutes, turning them over halfway through.

Calories 95	**Sodium** 155 mg	**EXCHANGES/ CHOICES**
Calories from Fat 30	**Potassium** 50 mg	1 Starch
Total Fat 3.5 g	**Total Carbohydrate** 13 g	1/2 Fat
Saturated Fat 0.4 g	**Dietary Fiber** 1 g	
Trans Fat 0.0 g	**Sugars** 1 g	
Cholesterol 15 mg	**Protein** 3 g	

FRESH VEGETABLE SUMMER ROLLS

SERVES 12 | SERVING SIZE: 1 ROLL

Fresh summer rolls are easy to make. Here, tofu replaces the Vietnamese shrimp filling for a vegetarian version of the classic and popular dish. All sorts of leftover shredded grilled or roast meats, such as chicken or pork loin, can take the place of the tofu, as can pre-cooked shrimp or crab. Feel free to experiment. Serve these as an appetizer or a main course with Spicy Peanut Sauce (page 13) for dipping.

1 head Boston or oak leaf lettuce, ribs removed (12 leaves)

1 pound firm tofu, drained and cut into 1/2-inch-thick matchsticks, lengthwise

1 large carrot, peeled and shredded

1/2 English hothouse cucumber, peeled, seeded, and julienned into 2-inch-long pieces

2 cups mung bean or clover sprouts, blanched

24 medium to large mint leaves

12 round rice papers (8-inch rounds)

Spicy Peanut Sauce (page 13)

1 Fill a flat round cake pan with water. Place a clean, smooth (not fuzzy) kitchen towel on your work surface. Arrange the lettuce, tofu, carrots, cucumber, sprouts, and mint into individual piles on a plate.

2 Put 1 rice paper in the water and soak until pliable. Place the rice paper on top of the kitchen towel and blot dry. The paper should be sticky, not slippery. Stack the ingredients one on top of the other on the side of the paper closest to you: 1 lettuce leaf, 1 piece of tofu, some carrot, cucumber, sprouts, and 2 mint leaves, one next to the other.

3 Fold the paper that is closest to you over the filling tightly, but be careful not to tear. Fold in the sides, and roll all the way to the end. Repeat this step with the remaining ingredients. Serve with Spicy Peanut Sauce (page 13) on the side.

VARIATION

Tofu is already cooked and ready to eat when purchased. However, if you would like to deepen the flavor, slice the tofu into 1/2-inch-thick slices, and pan-fry them in a nonstick skillet over medium heat. Add 2 tablespoons vegetable oil, and cook the tofu until golden crisp on both sides, about 4 minutes total. Drain on a paper-lined plate, and proceed with the recipe.

Calories 85
  Calories from Fat 20
Total Fat 2.0 g
  Saturated Fat 0.4 g
  Trans Fat 0.0 g
Cholesterol 0 mg

Sodium 55 mg
Potassium 155 mg
Total Carbohydrate 13 g
  Dietary Fiber 1 g
  Sugars 2 g
Protein 5 g

EXCHANGES/ CHOICES
1 Starch

SHITAKE AND ASPARAGUS SUSHI ROLLS

SERVES 12 | SERVING SIZE: 1 ROLL

Sushi is easy to make at home and requires very few ingredients. While you can serve sushi with the ubiquitous soy sauce and wasabi (Japanese horseradish), try them with the Walnut-Miso Sauce (page 10) for something unexpected, yet delicious. ***Tip:*** *Though you can make these rolls without any special equipment, using a bamboo sushi-rolling mat will make the job easier. Be sure to wrap the mat in plastic before using, to keep the rice from sticking to it.*

3 tablespoons rice vinegar

1 tablespoon agave nectar

Freshly-made Basic Brown Rice ("Sushi," page 61)

24 grilled, sautéed, or steamed asparagus spears

2 large Haas avocado, halved, pitted, peeled, and sliced into 12 equal wedges

12 large fresh shitake mushrooms, stems removed, caps julienned

12 nori seaweed sheets

Walnut-Miso Sauce (page 10)

1   In a medium mixing bowl, whisk together the vinegar and agave nectar until well combined. Add the rice, and mix thoroughly. Spread the rice evenly in a baking dish. Divide into 6 portions.

2   Arrange the ingredients on a large plate in individual piles including the asparagus, avocado, and shitakes. Place a bowl of water next to the rice.

3   Place a sheet of nori on top of a rolling mat. Dip your hand in water, and grab 1/2 cup of rice. Spread the rice throughout the nori sheet, corner to corner, but keep 2 inches at the top empty. On the end closest to you, layer the ingredients: 2 asparagus spears, 2 slices avocado, and some shitake, overlapping these to cover the length of the asparagus.

4   Take the side of the nori closest to you, and roll over once tightly, securing the ingredients. Fold over again, this time enclosing the ingredients entirely. Continue to roll to the end. Repeat step with remaining ingredients. To serve, cut each roll into 8 equal pieces and serve with Walnut-Miso Sauce (page 10) for dipping.

Calories 150	**Sodium** 15 mg	**EXCHANGES/ CHOICES**
Calories from Fat 45	**Potassium** 300 mg	1 Starch
Total Fat 5.0 g	**Total Carbohydrate** 23 g	1 Vegetable
Saturated Fat 0.9 g	**Dietary Fiber** 4 g	1 Fat
Trans Fat 0.0 g	**Sugars** 3 g	
Cholesterol 0 mg	**Protein** 5 g	

SPICY CRAB SUSHI ROLLS

SERVES 6 | SERVING SIZE: 1 ROLL

This spicy crab sushi roll is inspired by the popular spicy tuna version, available in most Japanese sushi restaurants. Drain the crabmeat before using in this recipe.

3 tablespoons rice vinegar

1 tablespoon agave nectar

3 cups freshly made Basic Brown Rice ("Sushi," page 61)

1 pound pasteurized crab, minced

1 tablespoon sesame oil

1 scallion, trimmed and minced

1 teaspoon sriracha

6 sheets nori seaweed

Light soy sauce

Wasabi

1 In a medium mixing bowl, whisk together the vinegar and agave nectar until well combined. Add the rice, and mix thoroughly. Spread the rice evenly in a baking dish. Divide into 6 portions.

2 In a separate bowl, mix together the crabmeat, sesame oil, scallion, and sriracha until well combined. Divide into 6 portions.

3 Place a nori sheet on top of a rolling mat. Dip your hand in water, and grab 1/2 cup rice. Spread the rice throughout the nori sheet, corner to corner, but keep 2 inches at the top empty. Spread one portion of the crab along the side closest to you. Fold nori over once tightly, securing the crabmeat. Fold over again, this time enclosing the crabmeat entirely. Continue to roll to the end. Repeat step with remaining ingredients.

4 Cut each roll into 8 equal pieces, and serve with soy sauce and wasabi for dipping.

		EXCHANGES/ CHOICES
Calories 235	Sodium 265 mg	2 Starch
Calories from Fat 40	Potassium 345 mg	2 Lean Meat
Total Fat 4.5 g	Total Carbohydrate 30 g	
Saturated Fat 0.8 g	Dietary Fiber 2 g	
Trans Fat 0.0 g	Sugars 4 g	
Cholesterol 105 mg	Protein 18 g	

ASIAN ROAST PORK SLIDERS

SERVES 6 | SERVING SIZE: 1 SLIDER

These ground pork patties are absolutely delicious served on a whole-wheat hamburger bun and topped with Spicy Asian Coleslaw (page 86) and a hint of hot sauce. Pan-fry the pork patties or grill them outdoors. Both versions are delicious and will quickly become a favorite at your next outdoor barbecue party.

1 1/2 pounds coarsely ground pork (96% lean)

1-inch piece ginger, finely grated

1 large garlic clove, peeled and finely grated

1 scallion, trimmed and minced

1 tablespoon light soy sauce

2 teaspoons dark sesame oil

1 teaspoon tapioca starch or cornstarch

6 whole-wheat hamburger buns

Spicy Asian Coleslaw (page 86)

Sriracha

1 In a medium bowl, mix together the pork, ginger, garlic, scallion, soy sauce, sesame oil, and tapioca starch. Shape into 6 individual patties.

2 In a dry nonstick skillet over medium heat, cook the pork patties to medium doneness and golden on both sides, about 7 minutes total. Serve on whole-wheat bun, topped with coleslaw and sriracha, if desired.

Calories 280	**Sodium** 365 mg	**EXCHANGES/ CHOICES**
Calories from Fat 80	**Potassium** 480 mg	1 1/2 Starch
Total Fat 9.0 g	**Total Carbohydrate** 24 g	4 Lean Meat
Saturated Fat 2.1 g	**Dietary Fiber** 3 g	
Trans Fat 0.0 g	**Sugars** 4 g	
Cholesterol 60 mg	**Protein** 28 g	

BEEF SATAY

SERVES 12 | SERVING SIZE: 1 SKEWER

Satay, the Asian version of the Middle-Eastern kebob, can be seasoned with any number of spices. Here, curry powder provides the main flavor profile. Satay can be served with a side of rice and salad or grilled vegetables. Strip steak is used here, but feel free to use your favorite cut, or marinate a whole steak, such as hanger steak, sirloin, or fillet mignon.

1 cup light coconut milk

1 tablespoon Indian curry powder

1 tablespoon fish sauce

1 tablespoon agave nectar

1 large garlic clove, peeled and finely grated

1 piece ginger, peeled and finely grated

1 1/2 pounds strip steak, cut into long thin strips

12 long bamboo skewers, soaked in water for 1 hour

Spicy Fish Sauce Dressing (page 12)

Spicy Peanut Sauce (page 13)

1. In a medium mixing bowl, whisk together the coconut milk, curry, fish sauce, agave nectar, garlic, ginger, and strip steak. Let marinate for 1 hour at room temperature.

2. Preheat the grill to medium for 20 minutes. Thread the meat onto the skewers and grill to desired doneness or until crisp on the outside and pink on the inside (medium), about 5 minutes total. Serve with desired sauce.

Calories 75	**Sodium** 80 mg
Calories from Fat 20	**Potassium** 160 mg
Total Fat 2.5 g	**Total Carbohydrate** 1 g
Saturated Fat 1.2 g	**Dietary Fiber** 0 g
Trans Fat 0.0 g	**Sugars** 0 g
Cholesterol 30 mg	**Protein** 11 g

EXCHANGES/ CHOICES
2 Lean Meat

GRILLED BEEF IN GRAPE LEAVES ROLLS

SERVES 15 | SERVING SIZE: 2 ROLLS

Derived from a classic Vietnamese recipe, these morsels of ground beef wrapped in grape leaves and grilled are absolutely delightful when dipped in a sweet and sour fish sauce dressing. Serve these as an appetizer or over rice with refreshing Spicy Asian Coleslaw (page 86). Grape leaves, which are primarily used in Greek cooking, can be found in the international aisle of your supermarket. *Tip: Be sure to rinse and drain the grape leaves in several changes of water to get rid of the brine taste.*

1 pound ground beef (70% lean)

1 large shallot, peeled and minced

1 large garlic clove, peeled and minced

1 lemongrass stalk, trimmed, bruised leaves removed, and white to green stalk grated

1 tablespoon agave nectar

2 teaspoons fish sauce

30 medium grape leaves, soaked and drained

12 long bamboo skewers, soaked in water for 30 minutes

1 tablespoon vegetable oil

Spicy Fish Sauce Dressing (page 12)

1 Preheat the grill to high for 20 minutes. Meanwhile, in a medium bowl, mix together the beef, shallot, garlic, lemongrass, agave nectar, and fish sauce until well combined. Divide the mixture into 30 equal portions, and shape them into 2-inch-long sausages.

2 Place a grape leaf on top of a paper towel (to drain excess water), so the widest side is closest to you. Place a portion of meat on that end. Fold the widest side of the leaf over the meat. Fold in the sides, and continue to roll to the end. Repeat step with the remaining grape leaves and meat.

3 Place on skewers, about 1/2 inch apart. Thread 5 rolls on each of the "double" skewers. Brush with oil, and grill until cooked through and golden, 3 to 5 minutes, flipping once. Serve with dipping sauce.

		EXCHANGES/ CHOICES
Calories 80	Sodium 185 mg	1 Med-Fat Meat
Calories from Fat 45	Potassium 90 mg	
Total Fat 5.0 g	Total Carbohydrate 3 g	
Saturated Fat 1.5 g	Dietary Fiber 0 g	
Trans Fat 0.2 g	Sugars 1 g	
Cholesterol 15 mg	Protein 5 g	

CHICKEN SATAY

SERVES 6 | **SERVING SIZE: 3 SKEWERS**

Popular throughout Asia and elsewhere in the world, small morsels of meat are marinated, skewered, and grilled. In this version, the chicken is tenderized in a coconut-based marinade. Grilled until crisped on the edges, the skewered chicken is served with Spicy Peanut Sauce (page 13), with rice on the side and any number of pickled vegetables to complete the meal.

1 cup light unsweetened coconut milk

1/2 –1 Tbsp fish sauce fish sauce

2 teaspoons filtered water

1 tablespoon palm sugar or agave nectar

2 teaspoons Indian curry powder

1 large garlic clove, peeled and grated

1 ounce (1 1/2-inch piece) ginger, peeled and grated

1 pound boneless skinless chicken breast or thighs, thinly sliced

16 long bamboo skewers, soaked in water for 30 minutes

Spicy Peanut Sauce (page 13)

Spicy Asian Coleslaw (page 86)

Basic Brown Rice (page 61)

1 In a bowl, whisk together the coconut milk, fish sauce, water, palm sugar, curry, garlic, and ginger. Add the chicken, mixing well to distribute marinade throughout. Let stand for 1 hour.

2 Preheat grill to high heat for 20 minutes.

3 Meanwhile, divide the chicken, and thread onto the 16 bamboo skewers. Grill the chicken until cooked through and golden, about 8 minutes total. Serve with Spicy Peanut Sauce (page 13), Spicy Asian Coleslaw (page 86), and Basic Brown Rice (page 61).

Calories 95	Sodium 125 mg	**EXCHANGES/ CHOICES**
Calories from Fat 20	Potassium 165 mg	2 Lean Meat
Total Fat 2.5 g	Total Carbohydrate 1 g	
Saturated Fat 1.0 g	Dietary Fiber 0 g	
Trans Fat 0.0 g	Sugars 1 g	
Cholesterol 45 mg	Protein 16 g	

PORK SATAY

SERVES 12 | **SERVING SIZE: 1 SKEWER**

The most inexpensive and popular meat in Asia, pork is also very versatile. In this recipe, pork tenderloin is sliced, marinated, skewered, and grilled for satay. Simply wrapped in tender lettuce leaves with shredded carrots, cucumber, and mint, it makes for a light lunch or dinner, but feel free to add brown rice for a heartier meal.

2 cups light, unsweetened coconut milk

1 tablespoon Indian curry powder

2 tablespoons fish sauce

1 tablespoon agave nectar

1 large garlic clove, peeled and finely grated

1 piece ginger, peeled and finely grated

1 1/2 pounds pork tenderloin, thinly sliced diagonally

12 long bamboo skewers, soaked in water for 1 hour

Spicy Fish Sauce Dressing (page 12)

Spicy Peanut Sauce (page 13)

1 In a medium mixing bowl, whisk together the coconut milk, curry powder, fish sauce, agave nectar, garlic, ginger, and pork. Let marinate for 1 hour at room temperature.

2 Preheat the grill to medium for 20 minutes. Thread the meat onto the skewers, and grill to desired doneness or until crisp on the outside and pink on the inside (medium), about 5 minutes total. Serve with desired sauce.

Calories 65	**Sodium** 80 mg	**EXCHANGES/ CHOICES**
Calories from Fat 20	**Potassium** 205 mg	1 Lean Meat
Total Fat 2.0 g	**Total Carbohydrate** 1 g	1/2 Fat
Saturated Fat 1.0 g	**Dietary Fiber** 0 g	
Trans Fat 0.0 g	**Sugars** 0 g	
Cholesterol 30 mg	**Protein** 11 g	

PORK MEATBALLS

SERVES 24 | **SERVING SIZE: 1 MEATBALL**

No matter where you go in the world, there's always some kind of meatball as part of the local fare. This Vietnamese version is easy to make and perfect for taking on a picnic.

1 tablespoon fish sauce

1 tablespoon agave nectar

1 small shallot, peeled and grated

1 medium garlic clove, peeled and grated

1 lemongrass stalk, trimmed, bruised leaves removed, and white and green parts grated

Freshly ground black pepper

1 1/2 pounds pork shoulder, coarsely ground

1 tablespoon vegetable oil

Spicy Peanut Sauce (page 13)

1 In a large bowl, stir together the fish sauce, agave nectar, shallot, garlic, lemongrass, pepper to taste, and pork. Shape into 24 small meatballs.

2 In a nonstick skillet over medium heat, add the oil and cook the meatballs, rolling them around until golden and cooked through, about 7 minutes. Serve with Spicy Peanut Sauce (page 13).

Calories 60
  Calories from Fat 30
Total Fat 3.5 g
  Saturated Fat 1.1 g
  Trans Fat 0.0 g
Cholesterol 20 mg

Sodium 75 mg
Potassium 90 mg
Total Carbohydrate 1 g
  Dietary Fiber 0 g
  Sugars 1 g
Protein 6 g

EXCHANGES/ CHOICES
1 Med-Fat Meat

ASIAN SHRIMP SAUSAGES

SERVES 6 | SERVING SIZE: 5 SAUSAGES

The minute you try these lemongrass-infused shrimp sausages, you'll be hooked. Plump and perfectly seasoned, they are delicious wrapped in lettuce leaves with shredded carrots, sliced cucumber, and fresh mint leaves, and dipped in Spicy Fish Sauce Dressing (page 12) for a relatively light and refreshing meal.

2 cups brown jasmine rice

2 pounds headless, peeled and deveined tiger shrimp

2 tablespoons vegetable oil, divided use

2 teaspoons agave nectar

1 1/2 teaspoons baking soda

4 scallions, trimmed and minced

Low-sodium salt

Freshly ground black pepper

Spicy Fish Sauce Dressing (page 12)

1 In a dry skillet over medium heat, add the rice and toast it, shaking the pan occasionally so as not to burn the grains. Cook rice until deep golden, about 5 minutes. Let cool, transfer to a clean spice grinder, and process to a fine powder. Sift through a fine mesh sieve to collect only the fine powder. Process the remaining ground rice to a fine powder.

2 In a medium bowl, mix together the shrimp, 1/3 cup rice flour, 1 teaspoon oil, agave nectar baking soda, and scallions, and season lightly with salt and pepper, until well combined. Cover and refrigerate for 30 minutes. Divide shrimp into 30 portions, rolling each into 2-inch-long sausages.

3 Put the remaining rice flour on a plate and roll each shrimp sausage in the flour. Shake off excess flour.

4 In a large nonstick skillet over medium heat, add 1/2 the remaining oil and cook half the shrimp sausages rolling them around until golden on all sides, 3 to 5 minutes. Repeat step with remaining oil and shrimp sausages. Serve with Spicy Fish Sauce Dressing (page 12) on the side.

		EXCHANGES/ CHOICES
Calories 265	Sodium 700 mg	1 Starch
Calories from Fat 65	Potassium 380 mg	4 Lean Meat
Total Fat 7.0 g	Total Carbohydrate 16 g	
Saturated Fat 0.8 g	Dietary Fiber 1 g	
Trans Fat 0.0 g	Sugars 2 g	
Cholesterol 245 mg	Protein 34 g	

ABOVE: **PICKLED DAIKON, CABBAGE, CUCUMBER, AND CARROTS** | page 21
BELOW: **PICKLED CURRY-GARLIC JAPANESE CUCUMBERS** | page 22

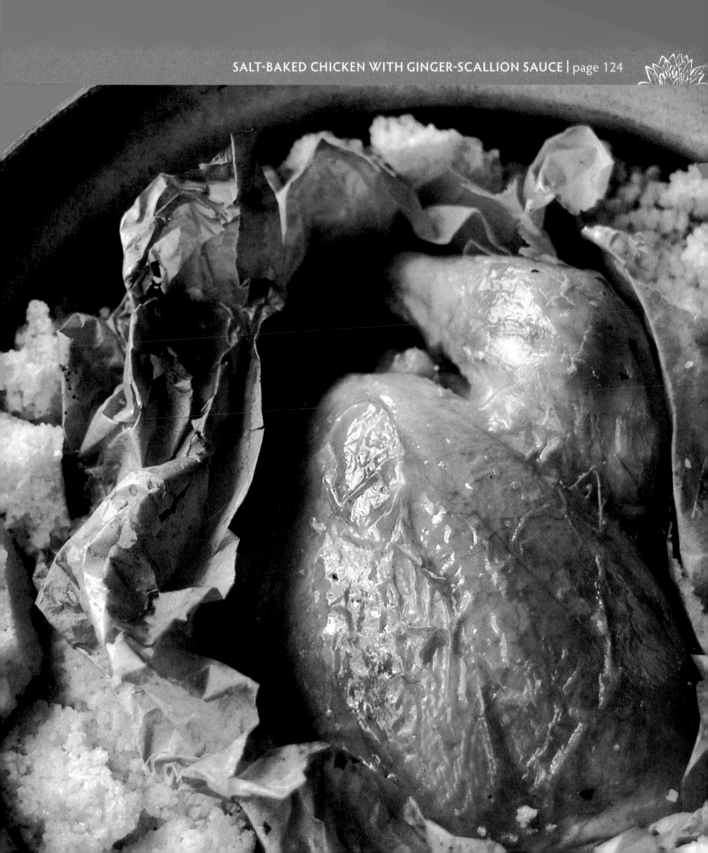

SCALLION SILVER DOLLARS

SERVES 6 | SERVING SIZE: 2 PANCAKES

Crisp on the outside and soft on the inside, these silver dollar pancakes are a smaller and healthier baked version of the classic, shallow-fried Chinese pancakes. This smaller, thicker version is a perfect compliment to the Pork Meatballs (page 55). Simply split the pancake in half and use it like a hamburger bun, placing a pork patty in the center, topped with pickled Daikon, Cabbage, Cucumber, and Carrots (page 21), or Spicy Asian Coleslaw (page 86). Scallion pancakes are also wonderful by themselves.

1 1/2 cups all-purpose flour

1 1/2 cup whole-wheat flour

1 teaspoon low-sodium salt

2 teaspoons baking powder

6 scallions, trimmed, white and green parts thinly sliced

1 cup spring or filtered water

1 tablespoon vegetable oil

1 tablespoon dark sesame oil

1 In a fine mesh sieve set over a bowl, sift the all-purpose and whole-wheat flours together.

2 In a large bowl, mix together 2 cups mixed flour, salt, and baking powder. Add the scallions and stir to blend. Make a well in the center and add the water, vegetable oil, and sesame oil. With a spoon, incorporate the dry and wet ingredients. Turn out the soft dough onto a floured work surface and knead, adding some or all of the remaining flour, until smooth and elastic, about 5 minutes. Wrap in plastic, and let rest 30 minutes at room temperature.

3 Preheat the oven to 375°F. Cut the dough into 12 equal balls. Flatten each ball into 1/4-inch thick disks and place them 1 inch apart on a parchment-lined cookie sheet. Bake until golden, about 15 minutes.

Calories 260	**Sodium** 260 mg	**EXCHANGES/ CHOICES**
Calories from Fat 45	**Potassium** 495 mg	3 Starch
Total Fat 5.0 g	**Total Carbohydrate** 47 g	1/2 Fat
Saturated Fat 0.6 g	**Dietary Fiber** 5 g	
Trans Fat 0.0 g	**Sugars** 1 g	
Cholesterol 0 mg	**Protein** 8 g	

CHAPTER FOUR
Rice, Noodles, and Crêpes

In Asia, a meal is not a meal without rice. Noodles and wheat-based products like crêpes are secondary and considered snacks.

Rice is often served plain, meaning unseasoned. It is frowned upon to season it at the table with soy sauce. Think of it this way: The rice is the canvas and backbone to every meal. It is what holds all the flavors together and therefore is considered the main dish. What Westerners would consider main dishes are actually sides of meat, fish, and vegetables. The "sides" are flavor enhancers, while the plain rice rounds out the flavors and allows them to fuse on the palate. Imagine if the rice were seasoned and served with seasoned sides. The meal would lack balance.

Fried rice is traditionally made with leftovers. Fried rice itself is a leftover because it is best made with one-day-old rice that has been cooled (or refrigerated) overnight, rendering the grains hard, and keeping them separated when stir-fried. This is important when cooked with all sorts of leftover meats, seafood, and/ or vegetables. Like many stir-fries, fried rice starts by seasoning your cooking vessel, adding oil, and stir-frying chopped garlic, ginger, and scallions. The leftover plain rice is then added and tossed to heat the grains evenly throughout. A raw egg is then added, for the sole purpose of adding a beautiful yellow hue to the grains. The rice is vigorously tossed about to distribute the egg throughout, just long enough to dry out the rice again before adding all sorts of chopped meats, seafood, and vegetables. One popular combination is cubed ham, baby shrimp, and peas. Fried rice is considered a full meal, but if you want a side, stir-fried greens are best to maintain a balanced meal.

Noodles are considered snack food in Asia, though nowadays they are served as quick single-dish meal options for breakfast, lunch, or dinner. Times have changed, and Asians are adapting to Western ways. Think of instant noodles as Asian fast food. Consider that all Asian noodles can be cooked in 3 to 5 minutes. The difference between Asian fast food and Western fast food is that there are no lines, Asian fast food costs less money, and, most importantly, a bowl of noodles adorned with sliced meat or seafood, leafy greens, and fresh herbs is the healthy choice.

Crêpes are popular and came to Asia as a direct influence from French Colonials in Indo-China, which included Vietnam, Cambodia, and Laos. The difference between a Vietnamese crêpe and the original French version is in the ingredients. Rice flour and coconut milk have replaced wheat flour and cow's milk. While Asian crêpes are generally savory, and they can also be filled with fruit. Like dumplings and spring rolls (see Finger Foods, page 39), once you have learned the technique, the possibilities for fillings are endless.

BASIC BROWN RICE (BASMATI, JASMINE, AND SUSHI)

SERVES 6 | SERVING SIZE: 1 CUP

Learning how to cook rice perfectly is incredibly important when preparing any Asian meal. Brown rice is high in fiber and far more nutritious than white rice. It is also forgiving when cooked, because it's hard to overcook. It retains a pleasant firm texture, along with a nutty flavor that is subtle and naturally sweet. Freshly made, it can be served as the main starch at any meal, or turned into delicious one-dish meals. Any leftover can be refrigerated and stir-fried the next day. ***Note:*** *sushi rice is especially excellent for making Brown Rice Congee with Stir-fried Herbs (page 36).*

1 1/2 cups brown rice (medium grain sushi, long grain jasmine, or basmati)

2 1/2 cups filtered water (2 cups for basmati)

1 In a heavy bottom pot, add the rice and water, cover, and bring to a boil over high heat. Reduce heat to medium-low, and cook until all of the water has been absorbed, about 20 minutes. Turn off the heat, let stand for 10 minutes, and fluff the grains. Serve hot or at room temperature.

Calories 160
  Cal ories from Fat 15
Total Fat 1.5 g
  Saturated Fat 0.3 g
  Trans Fat 0.0 g
Cholesterol 0 mg

Sodium 0 mg
Potassium 105 mg
Total Carbohydrate 34 g
  Dietary Fiber 2 g
  Sugars 1 g
Protein 4 g

EXCHANGES/ CHOICES
2 Starch

MINTY JASMINE RICE WITH CHICKEN

SERVES 6 | SERVING SIZE: 1 CUP

Served at room temperature with a sweet, savory, and tangy lime and fish sauce dressing drizzled generously on top, this relatively light and refreshing minty rice and chicken dish is perfect from late spring to early fall. Easy to assemble, the chicken comes from making the Asian Chicken Stock (page 17), but leftover steamed or roasted chicken also works well for this recipe. Serve this rice dish over a bed of greens for a healthy lunch or dinner.

3 cups Basic Brown Rice ("Jasmine," page 61), freshly cooked and warm

12 ounces (about 2 cups) shredded, cooked white or dark meat chicken

1 medium shallot, peeled and minced

12 large fresh mint leaves, freshly torn

Spicy Fish Sauce Dressing (page 12)

1. In a large bowl, mix together the Jasmine Brown Rice, chicken, shallot, and mint leaves. Divide among 6 servings, drizzling each with Spicy Fish Sauce Dressing (page 12) to taste (1 to 2 tablespoons recommended).

Calories 205	Sodium 50 mg
Cal ories from Fat 25	Potassium 210 mg
Total Fat 3.0 g	Total Carbohydrate 23 g
Saturated Fat 0.8 g	Dietary Fiber 2 g
Trans Fat 0.0 g	Sugars 1 g
Cholesterol 50 mg	Protein 20 g

EXCHANGES/ CHOICES
1 1/2 Starch
2 Lean Meat

GARLIC-CILANTRO JASMINE RICE

SERVES 6 | SERVING SIZE: 1 CUP

This is a delicious alternative to serving plain rice. Rich with ginger, garlic, and cilantro notes, it is a perfect complement to many Asian meals, and any leftovers make for an excellent and very fragrant fried rice.

2 tablespoons grapeseed or vegetable oil

2 large garlic cloves, peeled and finely chopped

1 ounce (1 1/2-inch piece) ginger, peeled and finely chopped

1 1/2 cups brown jasmine rice

3 cups Asian Chicken Stock (page 17)

1 whole bunch cilantro, lower stems trimmed

1 In a large pot over high heat, add the oil, and stir-fry the garlic and ginger until fragrant and golden, about 1 minute. Add the rice, and stir a few times to toast, about 1 minute. Add the stock, and scatter the cilantro on top. Cover and bring to a boil.

2 Reduce heat to medium-low, and cook until the rice has absorbed the liquid fully, about 25 minutes. Let stand for 5 minutes, and fluff before serving.

Calories 225	**Sodium** 15 mg
Cal ories from Fat 55	**Potassium** 235 mg
Total Fat 6.0 g	**Total Carbohydrate** 38 g
Saturated Fat 0.8 g	**Dietary Fiber** 3 g
Trans Fat 0.0 g	**Sugars** 1 g
Cholesterol 0 mg	**Protein** 5 g

EXCHANGES/ CHOICES
2 1/2 Starch
1 Fat

JEWELED BASMATI RICE WITH GOJI BERRIES

SERVES 6 | SERVING SIZE: 1 CUP

In many parts of Asia, rice is often garnished or mixed with ingredients to render the white grain more colorful. Exotic goji berries and shaved raw broccoli florets turn plain rice into a vegetarian course that can be served over fresh salad greens.

3 cups freshly cooked Basic Brown Rice ("Basmati," page 61)

1/3 cup goji berries

1/3 cup sunflower seeds

1 cup shaved raw broccoli florets

1/4 cup Fried Scallion Oil (page 20), (scallions only, drained)

8 large dates, pitted and chopped

2 tablespoons light soy sauce

1-inch ginger, peeled and grated

1 tablespoon dark sesame oil

3 tablespoons vegetable oil

Juice of 1 lemon (about 1/4 cup)

1 In a large bowl, mix together the rice, berries, seeds, broccoli, scallion oil, dates, soy sauce, ginger, sesame and vegetable oils, and lemon juice. Toss well and serve.

Calories 285	Sodium 195 mg
Cal ories from Fat 135	Potassium 270 mg
Total Fat 15.0 g	Total Carbohydrate 35 g
Saturated Fat 1.5 g	Dietary Fiber 4 g
Trans Fat 0.0 g	Sugars 8 g
Cholesterol 0 mg	Protein 5 g

EXCHANGES/ CHOICES
1 1/2 Starch
1/2 Fruit
3 Fat

STIR-FRIED SUSHI RICE WITH SHITAKES AND GARLIC

SERVES 6 | SERVING SIZE: 1 CUP

The key to a great fried rice is to cook the rice the day before, chill it overnight, and stir-fry it the next day. This will keep the rice grains separate and keep them from getting gummy. A classic in Asian food cultures, fried rice is a perfect way to use up leftovers, such as stir-fried vegetables, roast chicken, or grilled shrimp. The technique is quite simple, requires high heat, a large skillet, and constant tossing of the ingredients while cooking, in order to distribute the heat evenly throughout.

2 tablespoons grapeseed or vegetable oil

1 large garlic clove, crushed, peeled, and minced

1 ounce fresh ginger, peeled and minced

8 large shitake mushrooms, stems removed, caps julienned

3 cups day-old cooked and chilled brown sushi rice (short grain)

1 large egg, lightly beaten

1 tablespoon light soy sauce

2 teaspoons sesame oil

Freshly ground black pepper

1 In a large nonstick skillet over medium heat, add the oil and stir-fry the garlic, ginger, and mushrooms until fragrant and golden, about 2 minutes. Add the rice and egg, and continue to stir-fry, thoroughly incorporating the egg, until hot, about 10 minutes. Season with soy sauce and sesame oil, and black pepper to taste, and continue to stir-fry for 2 minutes more. Serve hot.

		EXCHANGES/ CHOICES
Calories 195	**Sodium** 155 mg	1 1/2 Starch
Cal ories from Fat 70	**Potassium** 110 mg	1 Vegetable
Total Fat 8.0 g	**Total Carbohydrate** 27 g	1 1/2 Fat
Saturated Fat 1.1 g	**Dietary Fiber** 2 g	
Trans Fat 0.0 g	**Sugars** 1 g	
Cholesterol 30 mg	**Protein** 4 g	

FRIED RICE WITH SHRIMP, PORK, AND GREEN PEAS

SERVES 6 | SERVING SIZE: 1 CUP

Fried rice is a classic meal made with leftover rice, the grains having dried out just enough to ensure they separate nicely when stir-fried. Use any kind of rice, brown sushi for a hearty chewy version, or the lighter jasmine brown rice, or lighter yet basmati brown rice. All will do, giving you different textural results. All sorts of proteins and vegetables are used, so while this recipe calls for fresh shrimp, pork, and green peas, feel free to substitute leftover chicken, broccoli, and mushrooms.

2 tablespoons light soy sauce

2 teaspoons dark sesame oil

1 teaspoon sriracha (chili-garlic sauce)

1 8 ounce boneless pork chop, thinly sliced against the grain

2 tablespoons grapeseed or vegetable oil

1 ounce ginger, peeled and grated

1 large garlic clove, peeled and grated

18 medium headless and peeled tiger shrimp, halved lengthwise and deveined

4 cups day-old or chilled cooked Basic Brown Rice (page 61)

1 cup green peas

2 scallions, trimmed and thinly sliced

1 In a medium bowl, stir together the soy sauce, sesame oil, and sriracha. Add the pork and mix well.

2 In a large nonstick skillet, add the grapeseed oil and stir-fry the ginger and garlic until just golden, about 30 seconds. Add the pork and stir-fry until just cooked, about 2 minutes. Add the shrimp and cook until just done, about 1 minute. Add the rice and continue to stir-fry until heated through, about 3 minutes. Add the green peas and continue to stir-fry until cooked, about 1 minute more.

3 Serve in individual bowls, garnished with scallions.

		EXCHANGES/CHOICES
Calories 365	Sodium 360 mg	2 1/2 Starch
Cal ories from Fat 80	Potassium 445 mg	4 Lean Meat
Total Fat 9.0 g	Total Carbohydrate 36 g	
Saturated Fat 1.6 g	Dietary Fiber 4 g	
Trans Fat 0.0 g	Sugars 2 g	
Cholesterol 155 mg	Protein 32 g	

BROWN RICE WITH DRIED FRUIT, SEEDS, AND NUTS

SERVES 6 | SERVING SIZE: 1 CUP

This recipe is a great way to use freshly cooked rice. It requires no additional cooking and is perfect served over a bed of greens or as a side to any meat or seafood protein. The Lemon-Miso Dressing (page 9) with a hint of hot sriracha gives the dish a nice spicy kick without overwhelming the palate. Pickled ginger is used to garnish the rice, refreshing the palate with every spoonful. This recipe is rich with nutrients because all ingredients are raw with the exception of the rice. **Tip:** *To "shave" broccoli florets, thinly slice the head of each stalk.*

3 cup cooked Basic Brown Rice
("sushi," page 61)

1/2 cup dried tart cherries

1/2 hothouse cucumber, peeled
(optional) and diced

1/4 cup raw sunflower seeds

1/2 cup raw crushed walnuts

1 cup shaved broccoli florets,
(3 stalks)

1/3 cup tightly packed fresh mint
leaves, chopped

1/3 cup Lemon-Miso Dressing
(page 9)

1 sprig mint, leaves only

1 In a large bowl, toss together the rice, cherries, cucumber, sunflower seeds, walnuts, broccoli, and mint. Add the dressing and toss to distribute evenly.

2 Serve at room temperature, garnished with whole mint leaves.

Calories 325	**Sodium** 55 mg
Cal ories from Fat 160	**Potassium** 260 mg
Total Fat 18.0 g	**Total Carbohydrate** 38 g
Saturated Fat 1.8 g	**Dietary Fiber** 4 g
Trans Fat 0.0 g	**Sugars** 11 g
Cholesterol 0 mg	**Protein** 6 g

**EXCHANGES/
CHOICES**
1 1/2 Starch
1 Fruit
3 1/2 Fat

SOBA NOODLE SALAD WITH SHITAKES AND SPINACH

SERVES 6 | SERVING SIZE: 1 1/4 CUP

Soba noodles are made of buckwheat and wheat flours. A specialty of northern Japan, they are hearty, healthy, and nutty in flavor. They can be served cold or in a piping hot broth. This simple dish of soba with shitakes and spinach can be served at room temperature or slightly chilled over a bed of fresh greens and a side of Chicken Teriyaki (page 127). For a more hearty meal, feel free to add any leftover roasted chicken, pork, or beef. Soba noodles come pre-portioned in a package of 3, 4, or more. Figure 1 portion per person, otherwise when adding meat or seafood protein to this dish, use 3 portions of noodles to serve 4.

6 portions (8 ounces) soba noodles

3 tablespoons grapeseed or vegetable oil, divided use

12 large shitake mushrooms, stems removed and caps julienned

1 pound baby spinach

1 1/2 tablespoons light soy sauce

2 tablespoons rice vinegar

2 teaspoons dark sesame oil

1 teaspoon local honey or agave nectar

1 teaspoon wasabi paste or sriracha (optional)

1 scallion, trimmed and thinly sliced

1/3 cup drained and tightly packed pickled ginger

Toasted sesame seeds

1 Bring a medium pot filled with water to boil over high heat. Add the noodles and cook until *al dente*, about 3 minutes. Drain and shock under cold running water or in an ice bath (water and ice mixed). Drain well and transfer to a mixing bowl.

2 In a large skillet or wok over high heat, add 2 tablespoons grapeseed oil and stir-fry the mushrooms until just wilted, about 1 minute. Add the spinach and continue to stir-fry until just wilted, about 1 minute more. Add to the noodles.

3 In a bowl, whisk together the remaining grapeseed oil, soy sauce, vinegar, sesame oil, honey, and wasabi. Drizzle over the noodles, tossing to mix the ingredients well. Divide among 6 individual portions, and garnish with some scallion, pickled ginger, and sesame seeds.

Calories 220	**Sodium** 395 mg	**EXCHANGES/ CHOICES**
Cal ories from Fat 80	**Potassium** 515 mg	1 1/2 Starch
Total Fat 9.0 g	**Total Carbohydrate** 31 g	2 Vegetable
Saturated Fat 1.0 g	**Dietary Fiber** 3 g	1 1/2 Fat
Trans Fat 0.0 g	**Sugars** 4 g	
Cholesterol 0 mg	**Protein** 8 g	

STIR-FRIED GLASS NOODLES WITH BEEF AND SPINACH

SERVES 6 | SERVING SIZE: 1 1/4 CUP

This noodle stir-fry uses Korean sweet potato starch noodles, which have the thickness of spaghetti and are translucent gray when dried, and transparent when cooked through. Gluten-free, they are flavorless but have the ability to absorb a great deal of flavor from other ingredients or sauces. This is a version of the classic Korean Chap Chae, stir-fried glass noodles with beef, spinach, and carrots for added texture, flavor, and color.

3 tablespoons light soy sauce, divided use

1 tablespoon dark sesame oil, divided use

8 ounces sirloin steak, thinly sliced

2 tablespoons grapeseed oil, divided use

2 large garlic cloves, peeled and minced

2-inch piece ginger, peeled and minced

1 large carrot, peeled and cut into 2-inch matchsticks

1 pound fresh baby spinach

1 1/4 cup Asian Chicken Stock (page 17), or filtered water

12-ounce package sweet potato starch noodles, soaked in water until pliable

1 In a medium bowl, stir together 1 tablespoon soy sauce and 1/2 teaspoon dark sesame oil. Add the steak and mix well.

2 In a large nonstick skillet, add 1 tablespoon grapeseed oil, and stir-fry 1/2 the garlic and ginger over medium heat. Add the beef, and stir-fry until pink, about 3 minutes. Transfer to a plate. Add the carrots to the same skillet, and cook for 1 minute. Add the spinach, and continue to stir-fry until just wilted, about 1 minute.

3 Transfer vegetables to the same plate. Add the remaining oil, garlic, ginger, soy sauce, sesame oil, chicken stock, and noodles to the skillet. Cook, stirring continuously, until the noodles have absorbed all liquid, about 5 minutes.

4 Return beef, carrots, and spinach to skillet, and toss to mix well.

Calories 345	Sodium 395 mg	**EXCHANGES/ CHOICES**
Cal ories from Fat 80	Potassium 620 mg	3 1/2 Carbohydrate
Total Fat 9.0 g	Total Carbohydrate 56 g	1 Lean Meat
Saturated Fat 1.4 g	Dietary Fiber 3 g	1 Fat
Trans Fat 0.0 g	Sugars 2 g	
Cholesterol 15 mg	Protein 11 g	

BRAISED GLASS NOODLES WITH CHICKEN AND NAPA CABBAGE

SERVES 6 | SERVING SIZE: 1 1/4 CUP

Chinese glass noodles, made of mung bean starch, are often labeled "bean thread." They absorb all sorts of delicious flavors from the stock and seasonings, as well as meats and vegetables that they're combined with.

2 tablespoons grapeseed oil

1 large garlic clove, peeled and minced

1-inch piece ginger, peeled and julienned

6 large napa cabbage leaves, cut into 1-inch strips

12 ounces skinless and boneless chicken breast, thinly sliced

1 1/2 cups Asian Chicken Stock (page 17) or store-bought low-sodium chicken stock

2 tablespoons light soy sauce

1 tablespoon dark sesame oil

2 0.7-ounce packages mung bean starch noodles ("bean thread"), soaked in water until pliable

2 scallions, trimmed and thinly sliced diagonally

1 In a medium heavy-bottom pot over high heat, add the oil and stir-fry the garlic and ginger until fragrant. Add the chicken and stir-fry until just opaque, about 3 minutes. Transfer to a plate.

2 Add the Napa cabbage and continue to stir-fry until just wilted, about 3 minutes. Transfer to the same plate. Add the stock, soy sauce, sesame oil, and noodles.

3 Reduce the heat to low, scatter the cabbage and chicken on top, and cook, covered, until the noodles have absorbed all the liquid, about 5 minutes. Toss well and serve hot, garnished with scallions.

		EXCHANGES/ CHOICES
Calories 165	**Sodium** 245 mg	1/2 Starch
Cal ories from Fat 70	**Potassium** 180 mg	2 Lean Meat
Total Fat 8.0 g	**Total Carbohydrate** 8 g	1 Fat
Saturated Fat 1.2 g	**Dietary Fiber** 0 g	
Trans Fat 0.0 g	**Sugars** 1 g	
Cholesterol 35 mg	**Protein** 13 g	

STIR-FRIED RICE NOODLES WITH CHICKEN AND BEAN SPROUTS

SERVES 6 | SERVING SIZE: 1 1/4 CUPS

Rice noodles are simple to cook and only require slightly more oil than other types of noodles so they do not stick together when stir-fried. Substitutes are easy to make as well. While chicken is used here, feel free to experiment with pork, shrimp, or both.

4 tablespoons grapeseed oil, divided use

1 large garlic clove, peeled and minced

1-inch piece ginger, peeled and minced

12 ounces boneless, skinless chicken thighs, thinly sliced

12 scallions, trimmed and cut into 1-inch pieces, white parts halved lengthwise

3 tablespoons light soy sauce

1 cup Asian Chicken Stock (page 17)

12 ounces dried rice sticks, soaked in water until pliable

4 cups bean sprouts

Sriracha (optional)

1 In a large nonstick skillet, add 2 tablespoons oil, and stir-fry the garlic and ginger over medium heat. Add the chicken and scallions and 1 tablespoon soy sauce, and cook until the chicken is cooked through opaque, about 5 minutes. Transfer to a plate.

2 In the same skillet, add the remaining oil, chicken stock, and rice noodles, stirring occasionally until the rice noodles have absorbed the liquid, about 7 minutes. Add the sprouts, and return the chicken to the skillet. Toss the ingredients together until well combined, about 1 minute. Serve hot in individual bowls or plates with sriracha.

		EXCHANGES/CHOICES
Calories 410	Sodium 440 mg	3 Starch
Cal ories from Fat 125	Potassium 330 mg	2 Vegetable
Total Fat 14.0 g	Total Carbohydrate 55 g	1 Lean Meat
Saturated Fat 2.2 g	Dietary Fiber 3 g	2 Fat
Trans Fat 0.0 g	Sugars 4 g	
Cholesterol 35 mg	Protein 16 g	

COCONUT RICE NOODLES WITH SHRIMP AND PEAS

SERVES 6 | SERVING SIZE: 1 1/4 CUP

Rice noodles are versatile and come in different sizes and shapes. Here, fine rice vermicelli complements the shrimp and peas perfectly. This dish is wonderful any time of the year. During winter, feel free to use a thicker noodle for a more substantial meal.

2 tablespoons grapeseed oil

1 large clove garlic, peeled and minced

1 large shallot, peeled and minced

1 tablespoon red Thai curry paste

1 teaspoon Indian curry powder or ground turmeric

36 medium headless, peeled and deveined tiger shrimp

1 cup light unsweetened coconut milk

1 cup Asian Chicken Stock (page 17), or filtered water

1 tablespoons fish sauce

8 ounces rice vermicelli, soaked until pliable

1 1/2 cups shelled peas, fresh or frozen

12 sprigs cilantro, stems trimmed

1 lime, cut into 6 wedges

1. In a large nonstick skillet, add the oil and stir-fry the garlic and shallots over medium heat until golden, about 3 minutes.

2. Add the curry paste and powder, and continue to stir-fry until fragrant and a shade darker. Add the shrimp, and continue to cook until just opaque, about 1 minute. Add the coconut milk, chicken stock, fish sauce, vermicelli, and peas, and cook until the noodles have absorbed all of the liquid, about 1 minute.

3. Divide among individual bowls or plates, and garnish with cilantro sprigs and lime wedge.

Calories 440
Cal ories from Fat 80
Total Fat 9.0 g
Saturated Fat 3.0 g
Trans Fat 0.0 g
Cholesterol 275 mg
Sodium 810 mg
Potassium 610 mg
Total Carbohydrate 44 g
Dietary Fiber 4 g
Sugars 4 g
Protein 42 g

EXCHANGES/ CHOICES
3 Starch
5 Lean Meat

PAN-FRIED EGG NOODLES WITH SHRIMP, SCALLOPS, AND SQUID

SERVES 6 | SERVING SIZE: 1 1/4 CUP

Egg noodles are popular and similar to Italian pasta, though definitely more egg-y in flavor. Available in all shapes and sizes in Asian markets, some can also be found in the international aisle of supermarkets. A classic Chinese dish, this double-cooked noodle, first boiled, then pan-fried until crisp, is topped with a seafood stir-fry. This dish is very versatile, so feel free to top these double-cooked noodles with any kind of stir-fry combination.

1 pound fresh round egg noodles, or 4 "cakes" instant dried egg noodles

1/4 cup grapeseed oil, divided use

1 large garlic clove, peeled and minced

1-inch piece ginger, peeled and minced

3 scallions, trimmed and cut into 1-inch pieces, white parts halved lengthwise

12 medium headless, peeled and deveined tiger shrimp, halved lengthwise

6 large sea scallops, halved on the bias

2 cleaned large squids, tentacles separated and bodies cut into 1/2-inch rings

1 cup Asian Chicken Stock (page 17)

2 tablespoons light soy sauce

1 tablespoon oyster sauce

1 teaspoon chili-garlic sauce (optional)

1 tablespoon dark sesame oil

1 teaspoon tapioca starch or cornstarch diluted with 1 tablespoon water

6 sprigs cilantro, trimmed

1 Bring a medium pot of water to a boil over high heat. Add the noodles, and boil until *al dente*, about 2 minutes for either fresh or dried, which are already pre-cooked. Drain and transfer to a plate. Shape the noodles into an even round layer, the size of an 8-inch dinner plate.

2 In a large nonstick skillet over medium heat, add 2 tablespoons oil, and slide the egg noodle "cake" into it. Cook until golden, about 3 minutes. Slide onto a plate, flip, and slide back into the skillet. Cook until golden, about 3 minutes. Slide back onto a serving platter.

3 In the same skillet, add the remaining oil, and stir-fry the garlic, ginger, and scallions until fragrant and lightly golden, about 2 minutes. Add the shrimp, scallops, and squid, and continue to stir-fry until just cooked, about 1 minute. Add the chicken stock, soy sauce, oyster sauce, chili-garlic sauce, and sesame oil. Add the tapioca starch mixture, stir, and continue cooking the seafood until the shrimp turns opaque, about 3 minutes. Spoon the seafood and sauce on top of the crispy noodles, and serve garnished with cilantro.

Calories 505	**Sodium** 575 mg	
Cal ories from Fat 160	**Potassium** 470 mg	
Total Fat 18.0 g	**Total Carbohydrate** 47 g	
Saturated Fat 1.8 g	**Dietary Fiber** 3 g	
Trans Fat 0.0 g	**Sugars** 1 g	
Cholesterol 410 mg	**Protein** 43 g	

EXCHANGES/ CHOICES
3 Starch
5 Lean Meat
1 Fat

SINGAPORE NOODLES WITH SHRIMP AND PORK

SERVES 6 | SERVING SIZE: 1 1/4 CUPS

"Singapore noodles" are a popular dish in Chinese-American restaurants. While they are traditionally made with Cantonese roast pork, which can be purchased in Asian markets or restaurants, feel free to use Canadian bacon or thick-cut ham in a pinch. This dish is also perfect with leftover chicken or beef.

2 tablespoons grapeseed oil

1 large garlic clove, peeled and minced

1 small yellow onion, peeled and sliced into thin wedges

24 small headless, peeled, deveined shrimp

6 ounces, thick-cut ham, diced into 1/4-inch pieces

1 tablespoon curry powder

12 ounces rice vermicelli, soaked in water until pliable

1 cup shelled peas, fresh or frozen

Low-sodium salt

Pepper

12 sprigs cilantro, stems trimmed

1 In a large skillet, add the oil and stir-fry the garlic and onions over medium heat until fragrant and golden, about 3 minutes. Add the shrimp, and cook until opaque, 1 to 2 minutes. Add the ham, and sprinkle with curry powder, tossing to distribute the spices. Add the noodles with 1/4 cup water, add the peas, and toss well until the noodles have absorbed all of the water, about 2 minutes. Adjust seasoning with salt and pepper to taste.

2 Serve hot in individual bowls or plates, and garnish with cilantro sprigs.

Calories 365	**Sodium** 445 mg	**EXCHANGES/ CHOICES**
Cal ories from Fat 65	**Potassium** 270 mg	4 Starch
Total Fat 7.0 g	**Total Carbohydrate** 58 g	1 Lean Meat
Saturated Fat 1.1 g	**Dietary Fiber** 4 g	1/2 Fat
Trans Fat 0.0 g	**Sugars** 3 g	
Cholesterol 45 mg	**Protein** 15 g	

COCONUT CRÊPES WITH SHITAKE MUSHROOMS AND PORK

SERVES 6 | **SERVING SIZE: 1 CRÊPE**

Coconut and rice flour crêpes are popular in Vietnam. Once you've mastered the technique of making these beautiful, thin pan-crisped crêpes, you can create all sorts of fillings. Wrapped in refreshing lettuce leaves and dipped in a sweet, sour, and savory fish sauce-based dressing, this is a perfect Summer dish.

1/2 cup rice flour

1/2 teaspoon turmeric

2/3 cup light unsweetened coconut milk

1/3 cup water

2 tablespoons grapeseed oil, divided use

1 scallion, trimmed and minced

12 ounces pork tenderloin, thinly sliced against the grain

1 pound fresh shitake mushrooms, stems discarded, caps julienned

12 large leaves, Boston or oak leaf lettuce

1 large carrot, peeled and julienned

1/2 hothouse cucumber, halved lengthwise and thinly sliced crosswise

6 sprigs mint

Spicy Fish Sauce Dressing (page 12)

1 In a bowl, whisk together the flour, turmeric, coconut milk, 1/3 cup water, 1 tablespoon oil, and scallions.

2 In a large skillet, add the remaining oil and stir-fry the pork over high heat until cooked through, about 2 minutes. Add the shitakes, and cook until just wilted, about 1 minute. Transfer to a plate.

3 In a well-oiled medium nonstick skillet, add 1/3 cup batter, swirl it around to cover the bottom of the pan, and cook over medium heat. Let set. Add some pork and shitakes. Fold in half, as you would an omelet. Slide onto a plate. Repeat 5 more times.

4 To serve, arrange the lettuce, carrots, cucumber, and mint leaves in individual piles on a large platter. Divide dipping sauce among 6 small bowls. To eat, take a lettuce leaf and fill it with some carrot, cucumber, and fresh mint. Tear apart crêpes and place inside the lettuce leaf. Wrap it all up tight and dip in the Spicy Fish Sauce Dressing (page 12).

		EXCHANGES/ CHOICES
Calories 200	Sodium 40 mg	1/2 Starch
Cal ories from Fat 70	Potassium 420 mg	2 Vegetable
Total Fat 8.0 g	Total Carbohydrate 20 g	1 Lean Meat
Saturated Fat 2.4 g	Dietary Fiber 2 g	1 1/2 Fat
Trans Fat 0.0 g	Sugars 3 g	
Cholesterol 30 mg	Protein 14 g	

COCONUT CRÊPES WITH MUNG BEAN SPROUTS AND SHRIMP

SERVES 6 | SERVING SIZE: 1 CRÊPE

Crêpes are popular around the world. Once you've learned this basic recipe and have mastered the art of swirling the batter around the pan, you can stuff them with anything, including sweet or savory fillings.

1/2 cup rice flour

1/2 teaspoon turmeric

1 cup light unsweetened coconut milk

2 tablespoon grapeseed oil, plus more for cooking, divided use

1 scallion, trimmed and minced

24 small headless, peeled and deveined tiger shrimp (about 1 pound)

1 1/2 pounds mung bean sprouts, root ends trimmed,

1 head lettuce

1 large carrot

1/2 hothouse cucumber, halved lengthwise and thinly sliced crosswise

6 sprigs mint

Spicy Fish Sauce Dressing (page 12)

1 In a bowl, whisk together the flour, turmeric, coconut milk, 1 tablespoon oil, and scallions.

2 In a large skillet, add the remaining oil, and stir-fry the shrimp over high heat, until opaque, about 1 minute. Add the mung bean sprouts and cook until just wilted, about 1 minute. Transfer to a plate.

3 In a well-oiled medium nonstick skillet over medium heat, add 1/3 cup batter, and swirl it around to cover the bottom of the pan. Let set. Add some shrimp and mung bean sprouts. Fold in half, as you would an omelet. Slide onto a plate. Repeat 5 more times.

4 Arrange the lettuce, carrots, cucumber, and mint leaves in individual piles on a large platter. Divide dipping sauce among 6 small bowls. Fill a lettuce leaf with some carrot, cucumber, and fresh mint. Tear apart crêpes and place inside the lettuce leaf. Wrap it all up tight, and dip in Spicy Fish Sauce Dressing (page 12).

		EXCHANGES/ CHOICES
Calories 235	Sodium 215 mg	1/2 Starch
Cal ories from Fat 70	Potassium 525 mg	2 Vegetable
Total Fat 8.0 g	Total Carbohydrate 21 g	2 Lean Meat
Saturated Fat 2.8 g	Dietary Fiber 3 g	1 Fat
Trans Fat 0.0 g	Sugars 6 g	
Cholesterol 120 mg	Protein 22 g	

CHAPTER FIVE
Vegetables

Vegetables grow abundantly in Asia. As a result, they are inexpensive and probably the most popular food. All meals in Asia include one or more vegetables, either pickled, stir-fried, or braised. Animal proteins, because they are expensive, are used in small quantities and considered flavor enhancers. You'll never see a steak in front of a guest at the table. Instead, that steak will be thinly sliced to serve many guests or will end up in the wok with all sorts of vegetables for stir-frying. The same goes for pork and seafood. All foods are shared, and the vegetables are the most important of all. A meal containing 70% or more vegetables is considered a balanced meal.

While steaming and stir-frying are the quickest and healthiest ways to cook vegetables, braised vegetables like Thai eggplant curry, for example, are well worth a try. Thai coconut curries are a great way to try all sorts of green vegetables. If your guests are not vegetable fans, a Thai coconut curry will easily change their minds. After all, who can turn down a creamy, spicy, coconut sauce spooned over rice?

Asian vegetables, like baby bok choy, daikon, and shitake mushrooms, are also delicious served in a clear chicken or pork broth. Adding thinly sliced scallions and ginger will enhance the flavor. Pair vegetables with a bowl of rice on the side, and you have all the fixings for a delicious and simple meal during the colder months of the year.

Be sure to always include vegetables at every meal. In Asia, there is no difference between breakfast, lunch, or dinner. There are no special foods reserved for different parts of the day. Each meal always includes a vegetable or two, a small amount of protein, and a bowl of rice. Oftentimes, it also includes a broth for sipping. Every meal is the same. It is all about balance in texture, color, and flavor.

STIR-FRIED ASIAN GREENS

SERVES 6 | SERVING SIZE: 1 CUP

A good stir-fry is done over high heat. It is essential to dry vegetables thoroughly prior to stir-frying them, or they will get soggy, especially delicate leafy greens. Always start by seasoning your cooking vessel by stir-frying garlic, ginger, or scallion or a combination thereof, especially if it is a cast iron or spun steel wok. Stir-frying is one of the popular cooking techniques today. It's a quick and healthy cooking method that allows ingredients to retain most of their nutrients.

2 tablespoons grapeseed or vegetable oil

1 tablespoon minced ginger

1 large garlic clove, peeled and minced

1 scallion, trimmed and minced

1 pound baby bok choy, trimmed, leaves separated

1 tablespoon light soy sauce

1 teaspoon dark sesame oil

1 In a wok or skillet, add the oil, and stir-fry the ginger, garlic, and scallion over high heat, until fragrant and golden, about 1 minute. Add the bok choy, season with soy sauce, and stir-fry until just wilted, about 3 minutes. Drizzle with sesame oil, and serve with rice.

		EXCHANGES/ CHOICES
Calories 60	Sodium 135 mg	1 Fat
Calories from Fat 45	Potassium 185 mg	
Total Fat 5.0 g	Total Carbohydrate 2 g	
Saturated Fat 0.6 g	Dietary Fiber 1 g	
Trans Fat 0.0 g	Sugars 1 g	
Cholesterol 0 mg	Protein 1 g	

POACHED BABY BOK CHOY WITH MUSHROOM SAUCE

SERVES 6 | SERVING SIZE: 1 CUP

Baby bok choy, white or green stemmed, can be found in Asian markets, and on average measure 3 to 4 inches long. If you cannot find baby bok choy, feel free to use the mature version or any other vegetable, such as asparagus, broccoli, or sugar snap peas. Serve over Basic Brown Rice (page 61) for a wholesome meal.

3 tablespoons grapeseed oil, divided use

Pinch low-sodium salt

1 1/2 pounds baby bok choy, stems trimmed lightly

2 large garlic cloves, peeled and minced

2-inch piece ginger, peeled and minced

4 scallions, trimmed and cut into 1 1/2-inch pieces, white parts halved lengthwise

8 medium to large dried shitake mushrooms, soaked in water until soft, water reserved

1 teaspoon tapioca starch or cornstarch

2 cups Asian Chicken Stock (page 17)

1 tablespoon light soy sauce

2 teaspoons dark sesame oil

1 teaspoon chili-garlic sauce (optional)

1 Fill a medium-sized pot with water, add 1 tablespoon oil, salt, and bring to a boil over high heat. Add the bok choy, and cook until just wilted, 1 to 2 minutes. Drain and arrange bok choy on a plate.

2 Meanwhile, in a small nonstick pan, add the remaining oil, and stir-fry the garlic, ginger, and scallions over medium heat until fragrant and lightly golden, about 3 minutes. Add the shitakes and 1 cup reserved soaking water. Dilute the tapioca starch with the chicken stock and add to the pan along with soy sauce, sesame oil, and chili-garlic sauce (if using). Reduce heat to low, and simmer until the mushrooms have absorbed some of the liquid, and the sauce is somewhat thickened, about 10 minutes. Pour over bok choy, and serve hot.

Calories 115	Sodium 285 mg
Calories from Fat 70	Potassium 405 mg
Total Fat 8.0 g	Total Carbohydrate 9 g
Saturated Fat 0.9 g	Dietary Fiber 2 g
Trans Fat 0.0 g	Sugars 2 g
Cholesterol 0 mg	Protein 3 g

EXCHANGES/ CHOICES
2 Vegetable
1 1/2 Fat

ROASTED CURRY VEGETABLES

SERVES 6 | SERVING SIZE: 1 CUP

Roasted vegetables take on a whole new character when seasoned with curry powder. Fresh out of the oven or cooled to room temperature, the vegetables can be eaten as they are, or tossed in a sweet and savory Lemon-Miso Dressing (page 9) and served over a bed of crisp leafy greens like tender oak leaf or crunchy romaine. They make for a perfect lunch, dinner, or side dish.

1 large sweet potato, scrubbed and cut into 1 1/2-inch pieces

1 large parsnip, scrubbed and cut into 1 1/2-inch pieces

1 large red beet, scrubbed and cut into 1 1/2-inch pieces

24 Brussels sprouts, trimmed and halved

2 tablespoons grapeseed or olive oil

1 teaspoon curry powder

Low-sodium salt

Freshly ground black pepper

Lemon-Miso Dressing (page 9; optional)

1 Preheat the oven to 400°F for 20 minutes.

2 In a large mixing bowl, toss together the sweet potato, parsnip, beet, and Brussels sprouts with oil, curry powder, salt, and pepper to taste. Scatter the vegetables on a large baking sheet, and roast until tender and golden, about 30 to 45 minutes, depending on the vegetable. Beets take more time than Brussels sprouts.

3 Transfer to a serving dish. Drizzle Lemon-Miso Dressing (page 9) on top, and serve hot or at room temperature.

Calories 120	**Sodium** 35 mg
Calories from Fat 45	**Potassium** 530 mg
Total Fat 5.0 g	**Total Carbohydrate** 18 g
Saturated Fat 0.6 g	**Dietary Fiber** 4 g
Trans Fat 0.0 g	**Sugars** 5 g
Cholesterol 0 mg	**Protein** 3 g

EXCHANGES/ CHOICES
1/2 Starch
2 Vegetable
1 Fat

BRAISED EGGPLANT CURRY

SERVES 8 | **SERVING SIZE: 1 CUP**

This Thai-inspired coconut curry is an incredibly flavorful dish. It is essential to build it one ingredient at a time in order to deepen its flavor. While eggplant is used in this recipe, feel free to experiment with all sorts of vegetables, mixing them up if you'd like. Zucchini, bell peppers, bamboo, and mushrooms also fare well here. Serve over rice or noodles with stir-fried greens on the side, and a meat or seafood protein for a hearty, yet balanced meal.

2 tablespoons grapeseed oil

4 large garlic cloves, crushed and peeled

1 large shallot, peeled and cut into thin wedges

1-inch piece ginger, thinly sliced lengthwise

3 scallions, trimmed and cut into 1-inch pieces

1 1/2 tablespoons red Thai curry paste

2 teaspoons Indian curry powder

1 cup light unsweetened coconut milk

2 cups Asian Chicken Stock (page 17), or vegetable stock

1 large globe eggplant, cut into 2-inch pieces

1 tablespoon fish sauce

Juice of 1 lemon (about 1/4 cup)

1 tablespoon agave nectar

12 sprigs cilantro, stems lightly trimmed

1 In a large pot, add the oil and stir-fry the garlic, shallots, ginger, and scallions over medium-high heat until fragrant and lightly golden, about 3 minutes. Stir-in the curry paste and powder, and continue to stir-fry until a shade darker, about 1 minute. Add the coconut milk, stock, eggplant, fish sauce, lemon juice, and agave nectar. Bring to a boil.

2 Reduce heat to medium-low, cover, and cook until the eggplant is soft, about 20 minutes. Serve hot, garnished with cilantro.

Calories 100	Sodium 320 mg
Calories from Fat 55	Potassium 250 mg
Total Fat 6.0 g	Total Carbohydrate 12 g
Saturated Fat 1.9 g	Dietary Fiber 2 g
Trans Fat 0.0 g	Sugars 5 g
Cholesterol 0 mg	Protein 2 g

EXCHANGES/ CHOICES
2 Vegetable
1 Fat

GRILLED BABY EGGPLANT WITH MISO SAUCE

SERVES 6 | SERVING SIZE: 2 EGGPLANT HALVES WITH MISO SAUCE

Miso is a fermented soybean paste used in Japanese cuisine. Derived from Chinese bean pastes or sauces, variations also exist in Korea. Some miso pastes are smooth, while others are chunky. The darker they are, the saltier they are. Here shiro-miso, "white" miso is used for its sweet and savory character. This lemon-ginger sauce is excellent on grilled vegetables as well as grilled meats and seafood. Feel free to use it as a marinade as well.

6 Japanese eggplants, halved lengthwise

2 tablespoons shiro-miso

Juice of 1 lemon (about 1/4 cup)

1 tablespoon sake (optional)

2 teaspoons agave nectar

1 teaspoon sriracha

1 tablespoon dark sesame oil

3 tablespoons grapeseed or olive oil

1-inch piece ginger, peeled and finely grated

1 scallion, trimmed and minced

1. On a well-oiled grill pan, grill the eggplant halves over medium heat until golden and soft on the inside, 5 to 7 minutes (flipping once).

2. Meanwhile, in a small bowl, whisk together the shiro-miso, lemon, sake, agave nectar, and sriracha, until smooth. Add the sesame oil and grapeseed oil, and continue to whisk until well incorporated. Stir in the ginger and scallion. Drizzle over grilled eggplant, or serve on the side for dipping.

Calories 140	**Sodium** 130 mg	**EXCHANGES/ CHOICES**
Calories from Fat 90	**Potassium** 175 mg	1/2 Carbohydrate
Total Fat 10.0 g	**Total Carbohydrate** 14 g	1 Vegetable
Saturated Fat 1.0 g	**Dietary Fiber** 3 g	2 Fat
Trans Fat 0.0 g	**Sugars** 7 g	
Cholesterol 0 mg	**Protein** 2 g	

GRILLED ZUCCHINI WITH GINGER-SOY SAUCE

SERVES 6 | SERVING SIZE: 1 WHOLE QUARTERED ZUCCHINI

Zucchini is a popular vegetable that is mild in flavor. When selecting, be sure to choose them firm to the touch and small and slender. Smaller zucchini will retain their firm texture when cooked. The ginger-soy dressing is savory, tangy, and mildly spicy. It can be used as a dipping sauce or marinade as well.

6 slender zucchini, quartered lengthwise

2 tablespoons vinegar

3 tablespoons light soy sauce

2 teaspoons dark sesame oil

1-inch piece ginger, peeled and grated

1 scallion, trimmed and minced

1 In a well-oiled grill pan, grill the zucchini pieces over medium heat until golden on all sides and cooked through, but still firm, about 5 to 7 minutes. Transfer to a cutting board, and quarter each piece crosswise into approximately 1-inch pieces.

2 Meanwhile, in a large bowl, whisk together the vinegar, soy sauce, sesame oil, ginger, and scallion. Add the grilled zucchini and toss. Serve hot or at room temperature.

Calories 45
  Calories from Fat 20
Total Fat 2.0 g
  Saturated Fat 0.3 g
  Trans Fat 0.0 g
Cholesterol 0 mg

Sodium 290 mg
Potassium 350 mg
Total Carbohydrate 6 g
  Dietary Fiber 2 g
  Sugars 3 g
Protein 2 g

EXCHANGES/ CHOICES
1 Vegetable
1/2 Fat

RAW ZUCCHINI SALAD WITH PRUNES AND TAMARI DRESSING

SERVES 6 | SERVING SIZE: 1/2 CUP

Zucchini is excellent eaten raw, retaining its crunchy texture when julienned into long, thin strands. Tossed with sweet prunes and drizzled with a savory and tangy, honey-sweetened tamari-based salad dressing, it makes for a perfect appetizer or vegetable side to any roasted or grilled meats or seafood.

1 tablespoon lite tamari or soy sauce

1 teaspoon raw organic local honey

2 tablespoons rice vinegar

1 teaspoon dark sesame oil

2 1/2 tablespoons grapeseed or olive oil

4 medium zucchini, lightly chilled and julienned lengthwise

8 pitted prunes, thinly sliced

Freshly ground black pepper

1 In a small bowl, whisk together the tamari, honey, vinegar, sesame oil, and grapeseed or olive oil. Add the zucchini, prunes, and black pepper to taste. Toss and serve.

		EXCHANGES/ CHOICES
Calories 110	Sodium 265 mg	1/2 Fruit
Calories from Fat 65	Potassium 435 mg	1 Vegetable
Total Fat 7.0 g	Total Carbohydrate 13 g	1 1/2 Fat
Saturated Fat 0.7 g	Dietary Fiber 2 g	
Trans Fat 0.0 g	Sugars 8 g	
Cholesterol 0 mg	Protein 2 g	

WASABI-SPICED CELERIAC SALAD

SERVES 6 | SERVING SIZE: 1/2 CUP

Celeriac, or celery root, is underrated. Rarely is it seen on restaurant menus, and only occasionally does it seem to show up at the market. This recipe is derived from the French classic celeriac called "remoulade." This Asian-inspired version will complement any grilled meat. It can also be served over a bed of leafy greens for a light meal.

3 tablespoons rice vinegar

1 teaspoon wasabi

1 tablespoon shiro-miso (white miso)

1 tablespoon local honey or agave nectar

1/4 cup grapeseed oil

1 small celeriac, peeled and finely julienned or shredded (about 4 cups)

1/2 cup packed cilantro leaves (about 1/2 bunch)

1. In a medium mixing bowl, whisk together the rice vinegar, wasabi, miso, honey, and oil until emulsified. Add the celeriac and toss well. Let stand for 30 minutes to 1 hour, tossing every 15 minutes or so to soften the celeriac.

2. Toss in the cilantro leaves, leaving a few behind for garnishing, and serve at room temperature or slightly chilled.

Calories 65	**Sodium** 160 mg
Calories from Fat 10	**Potassium** 330 mg
Total Fat 1.0 g	**Total Carbohydrate** 14 g
Saturated Fat 0.1 g	**Dietary Fiber** 2 g
Trans Fat 0.0 g	**Sugars** 5 g
Cholesterol 0 mg	**Protein** 2 g

EXCHANGES/ CHOICES
1 Carbohydrate

SPICY ASIAN COLESLAW

SERVES 6 | **SERVING SIZE: 1/2 CUP**

Asian coleslaw has the look of the classic American version but is seasoned with a sweet and tangy fish sauce-based dressing, rendering it slightly spicy with fiery red Thai chilies. Serve as a refreshing side to grilled meats or seafood, or simply over Basic Brown Rice ("Jasmine," page 61) as a light lunch or dinner.

2 tablespoons fish sauce

1 tablespoon agave nectar

Juice of 1 lemon (1/4 cup juice)

2 fresh red Thai chilies, stems and seeds removed, and minced

1/2 small green cabbage, finely julienned or shredded (about 6 cups)

2 medium carrots, peeled and finely julienned or shredded (about 1 1/2 cups)

1/2 cup cilantro leaves

1 In a large bowl, whisk together the fish sauce, agave nectar, and lemon until well combined. Add the chilies, cabbage, and carrots and toss well. Let macerate for 1 hour, tossing every 15 minutes or so, to allow the flavors to redistribute evenly.

2 Drain, add the cilantro, and toss. Serve at room temperature or slightly chilled.

Calories 35	**Sodium** 260 mg
Calories from Fat 0	**Potassium** 235 mg
Total Fat 0.0 g	**Total Carbohydrate** 8 g
Saturated Fat 0.0 g	**Dietary Fiber** 3 g
Trans Fat 0.0 g	**Sugars** 5 g
Cholesterol 0 mg	**Protein** 1 g

EXCHANGES/ CHOICES
1 Vegetable

MIXED GREENS WITH AVOCADO AND PINK GRAPEFRUIT SALAD

SERVES 6 | **SERVING SIZE: 1 1/2 CUPS**

Adding in-season fruit to salads makes for a beautiful presentation as well as an unexpected flavor combination. Pink grapefruit during the winter, or blueberries during the summer, combined with creamy avocado, nuts, and seeds, will result in a healthful, and filling meal. Serve this salad alone or as a side dish. *Tip: For best results, use a shallow bowl, drizzle the dressing on top of the salad, and let stand for 15 minutes rather than tossing. This will allow the dressing to trickle down slowly among the ingredients and will keep the lettuce from getting soggy.*

1 tablespoon shiro-miso

3 tablespoons rice vinegar

1 teaspoon local honey

2 tablespoons grapeseed or olive oil

Low-sodium salt

Freshly ground black pepper

1 head green or red oak leaf lettuce, leaves separated and torn

6 sprigs cilantro, leaves only

1 ripe pink grapefruit, peeled, sectioned, and membrane removed

1 ripe Haas avocado, peeled, pitted, and cut into bite-size pieces

1 tablespoon raw sunflower seeds

1/3 cup chopped walnuts

1 In a small bowl, whisk together the miso, vinegar, honey, and oil until smooth. Adjust seasoning with salt and pepper to taste.

2 In a shallow bowl, scatter the lettuce, cilantro, and top with grapefruit, avocado, sunflower seeds, and walnuts. Drizzle the dressing evenly across the top, and season with pepper.

Calories 165	**Sodium** 65 mg	**EXCHANGES/ CHOICES**
Calories from Fat 115	**Potassium** 280 mg	1 Carbohydrate
Total Fat 13.0 g	**Total Carbohydrate** 11 g	2 1/2 Fat
Saturated Fat 1.5 g	**Dietary Fiber** 3 g	
Trans Fat 0.0 g	**Sugars** 5 g	
Cholesterol 0 mg	**Protein** 3 g	

PAN-CRISPED TOFU SALAD

SERVES 6 | SERVING SIZE: 2 PIECES

Already cooked when packaged, tofu can be served directly from the container after draining. For the cold version of this recipe, feel free to use Japanese-style firm "silken tofu." If you plan on pan-crisping the tofu, it is best to use firm tofu packed in water, which is Chinese in style and somewhat grainy in texture.

1 1/2 tablespoons grapeseed oil

1 1/2 pounds firm tofu, drained and cut into 1/2-inch thick slices

2 scallions, trimmed and thinly sliced on the diagonal

1-inch piece ginger, peeled and finely julienned (thread-like)

1 red Thai chili, stem and seeds removed, and thinly sliced into rings, or 1 teaspoon chili-garlic sauce

2 tablespoons light soy sauce

2 tablespoons rice vinegar

1/2 tablespoon dark sesame oil

1 In a large nonstick pan, add the oil and tofu slices in a single layer and cook over medium heat until golden crisp on both sides, about 5–7 minutes. Transfer to a platter, overlapping the tofu slices, and garnish with scallions, chili, and ginger across the top.

2 Meanwhile, in a small bowl, stir together the soy sauce, vinegar, and sesame oil, and drizzle over tofu.

		EXCHANGES/ CHOICES
Calories 130	**Sodium** 200 mg	1 Med-Fat Meat
Cal ories from Fat 80	**Potassium** 215 mg	1 Fat
Total Fat 9.0 g	**Total Carbohydrate** 4 g	
Saturated Fat 1.5 g	**Dietary Fiber** 1 g	
Trans Fat 0.0 g	**Sugars** 1 g	
Cholesterol 0 mg	**Protein** 10 g	

SOUR MANGO SALAD

SERVES 6 | **SERVING SIZE: 1/2 CUP**

Sour, sweet, salty, bitter, and spicy, mango salad is refreshing and goes with all sorts of grilled meats or seafood. Green mangoes are not readily available outside of Chinatowns or Asian markets. However, hard-to-the-touch unripe mangos are easily found in supermarkets. Unripe is the key. The harder the mango, the better the results.

2 tablespoons fish sauce

Juice of 1 lime or lemon (about 1/4 cup)

1 tablespoon agave nectar

1 teaspoon chili-garlic sauce

3 unripe mangos, peeled and shredded

12 large mint leaves, julienned

1/3 cup crushed plain roasted unsalted peanuts

1 In a large bowl, stir together the fish sauce, lime juice, agave nectar, and chili-garlic sauce. Add the mango and mint, and toss well.

2 Garnish with crushed peanuts and serve.

Calories 115
  Cal ories from Fat 25
Total Fat 3.0 g
  Saturated Fat 0.5 g
  Trans Fat 0.0 g
Cholesterol 0 mg

Sodium 475 mg
Potassium 225 mg
Total Carbohydrate 23 g
  Dietary Fiber 2 g
  Sugars 19 g
Protein 2 g

EXCHANGES/ CHOICES
1 1/2 Fruit
1/2 Fat

EDAMAME AND YELLOW CORN SALAD

SERVES 6 | SERVING SIZE: 1/2 CUP

This edamame (soy bean) and yellow corn salad is wonderful during the summer, when corn is in season. Nothing could be easier than throwing this salad together and serving it as a starter course. With shrimp on the side, it can easily become a light lunch.

1/2 cup rice vinegar

1 teaspoon low-sodium salt

1 teaspoon agave nectar

1 small red onion, peeled and sliced into thin wedges

1 pound shelled edamame

2 ears corn, kernels sliced off the cob

1/3 cup Lemon-Miso Dressing (page 9)

1 In a medium bowl, stir together the vinegar, salt, and agave nectar. Add the red onion, and toss to coat well. Let pickle for 2 hours, tossing every 15 minutes or so, to redistribute the ingredients.

2 In the meantime, fill a medium pot with water, and bring to a boil over high heat. Add the edamame with a pinch of salt, and cook until tender, yet firm, about 1 minute. Drain and shock under cold running water. Drain and transfer to a serving bowl. Add the corn and dressing, and toss well.

Calories 200	**Sodium** 125 mg	**EXCHANGES/ CHOICES**
Cal ories from Fat 110	**Potassium** 445 mg	1 Starch
Total Fat 12.0 g	**Total Carbohydrate** 18 g	1 Lean Meat
Saturated Fat 1.2 g	**Dietary Fiber** 5 g	1 1/2 Fat
Trans Fat 0.0 g	**Sugars** 5 g	
Cholesterol 0 mg	**Protein** 10 g	

BRAISED SPICY TOFU WITH NAPA CABBAGE AND SHITAKES

SERVES 6 | SERVING SIZE: 1 CUP

Derived from the Korean classic called "soon doo boo," this braised spicy tofu dish is one that you'll enjoy especially during the cooler months of the year. Along with brown sushi rice, the rich tofu protein, crunchy yet tender napa cabbage, and earthy shitake mushroom combine for a complete wholesome vegetarian meal.

2 tablespoons grapeseed oil

4 large garlic cloves, peeled and crushed

2-inch piece ginger, peeled and thinly sliced lengthwise

6 scallions, trimmed and cut into 1-1/2-inch pieces, white parts halved lengthwise

12 large dried shitake mushrooms, soaked in water until softened, 2 cups soaking water reserved

2 tablespoons light soy sauce

1 tablespoon dark sesame oil

1 teaspoon agave nectar

2 tablespoons Korean chili-bean paste

1/2 cup sake

8 large Napa cabage leaves, cut into 1-inch strips

1 1/2 pounds firm tofu (silken or regular), drained (if packed in water) and cut into 1-inch cubes

1. In a large pot, add the oil, and stir-fry the garlic and ginger over medium heat, until golden, about 1 minute. Add the scallions and continue to stir-fry until just softened. Add the mushrooms, reserved mushroom water, soy sauce, sesame oil, agave nectar, chili-bean paste, sake, and 1 cup water.

2. Bring to a boil, and reduce heat to medium-low. Add the cabbage, and cook until softened, about 5 minutes. Add the tofu, and cook until heated through, about 2 minutes.

Calories 200	Sodium 250 mg	**EXCHANGES/ CHOICES**
Cal ories from Fat 110	Potassium 450 mg	2 Vegetable
Total Fat 12.0 g	Total Carbohydrate 13 g	1 Med-Fat Meat
Saturated Fat 1.8 g	Dietary Fiber 3 g	1 1/2 Fat
Trans Fat 0.0 g	Sugars 2 g	
Cholesterol 0 mg	Protein 11 g	

TOFU TERIYAKI

SERVES 6 | SERVING SIZE: 1 CUP

Teriyaki is a popular Japanese restaurant-style dish that is all about the sauce. Once the sauce is mastered, the protein can be interchanged. Tofu has a unique earthy flavor, though many seem to describe it as "bland." In this classic dish, even the most skeptical guest will appreciate this delightful Asian specialty. Serve with Basic Brown Rice (page 61) on the side.

1 tablespoons grapeseed oil

2 large garlic cloves, peeled

2-inch piece ginger, thinly sliced lengthwise, 3 slices thinly julienned (thread-like)

3 scallions, trimmed, 2 crushed, 1 thinly sliced diagonally

1 (2 × 4 inches piece) kombu (kelp)

1/4 cup light soy sauce

1/2 cup sake

1/2 cup water

1 tablespoon dark sesame oil

2 teaspoons agave nectar

1 teaspoon tapioca starch diluted with 1 tablespoon water

2 pounds firm tofu (silken or regular), drained and cut into 1-inch cubes

1 In a small to medium saucepan, add the oil, and stir-fry the garlic and ginger over medium heat until golden, about 1 minute. Add the crushed scallions, kombu, soy sauce, sake, 1/2 cup water, sesame oil, and agave nectar, and bring to a boil.

2 Reduce heat to simmer, and reduce by 1/3, about 5 minutes. Add the tapioca starch mixture to thicken the sauce, stirring continuously. Add the tofu, and continue to cook for 2 minutes more. Serve hot.

Calories 185	Sodium 390 mg
Cal ories from Fat 100	Potassium 310 mg
Total Fat 11.0 g	Total Carbohydrate 8 g
Saturated Fat 1.9 g	Dietary Fiber 2 g
Trans Fat 0.0 g	Sugars 3 g
Cholesterol 0 mg	Protein 14 g

EXCHANGES/ CHOICES
1/2 Carbohydrate
2 Med-Fat Meat

CHAPTER SIX
Seafood

Seafood is, for the most part, inexpensive in Asia because of an overwhelming abundance, especially in coastal regions. It can be steamed, stir-fried, or braised. When it comes to Asian foods, the technique is always the same. Build the flavor, one layer at a time. The same goes for seafood!

In general, whole fish are fresher than fillets and well worth considering. Selecting fresh fish is easy. If it looks good, it generally is. Look for glossy skin and plump eyes. If the eyes are sunken in, and the skin is dull, move on. A fish that has a fishy or strong aroma is generally a bad fish. (The same goes for all seafood.) It should smell fresh with a subtle aroma.

CLEANING FISH MADE EASY

Cleaning and filleting fish is easy, but if you are squeamish about that particular task, simply have your fishmonger do it for you. If you're adventurous and you like to connect with the food before eating it, here are some tips: Hold the fish in one hand, belly side up. Take a paring knife and insert it in the belly, starting just below the mouth and running it through lengthwise along the belly until you can't anymore, which means you've reached the meaty tail end. Remove the innards, rinse, and pat dry with a paper towel.

FILLETING

Some prefer to serve fish whole, head to tail, while others could care less about the flavorful meat surrounding the cartilage in the head. If the latter is the case, hold the fish by the tail, and cut off the head. Consider saving the head and using it for fish stock.

To fillet the fish, hold it by its tail. It might be slippery, so be careful. Or, you can use a towel to hold it firmly. Hold down the tail tightly against your cutting board, and make an incision crosswise at the tail end. Be careful not to cut yourself. Once you made the incision, run the blade around the back of the fish, then go back and run it through again, snug against the central bone of the fish, while lifting the fillet. Flip the fish and do the same on the other side.

CLEANING SQUID

Cleaning squid can seem daunting, but it's quite simple. Pull out the tentacles, along with the transparent bone and innards, which generally follow effortlessly. The tentacles are edible, but the beak must be removed by squeezing the head in the center. The inside of the body should be scraped clean with a teaspoon so as not to cut it open. If the recipe calls for the body to be cut open, do so down the seam, then scrape the inside of the body and cut the squid into pieces.

SOAKING MOLLUSKS

Clams, mussels, and oysters require a few changes of water to remove sand. Use cold running water to do this. Let them soak in it for 20 minutes, then change the water once or twice. You can also scrub the shells clean. For mussels, pull the beards off around each shell.

DEALING WITH LOBSTERS AND CRABS

Boiling lobsters and crabs is easy. Make a court-bouillon by bringing a large pot of water to a boil with about 1/4 cup vinegar, with some salt and pepper. Add the lobsters or crabs to the water, head first, always. This ensures that they will remain still while cooking for 10 minutes on average. (Note: Placing them in a pot of cold water, while bringing it to a boil, ensures that they will try and escape. Not fun, for you or for them!)

To open cooked crabs, hold the meaty half with legs in one hand and the head in the other. Pry open like a book. The tomalley is absolutely delicious and can be used in enriching sauces.

To open a cooked lobster, twist the head and pull off. Take a fork and insert it far into the tail inside the shell, then simply pull out the meaty tail. Another way to get to the tail is by splitting it in half lengthwise and prying it open to reveal the meat.

If killing lobsters or crabs is too much for you to handle, ask your fishmonger, who often gives you the option to buy these already boiled or steamed.

A PERFECT SAUCE

When it comes to boiled or steamed seafood, the most common dipping sauce is horseradish- and ketchup-based, which is often referred to as "cocktail sauce."

A great Southeast Asian-style sauce can be made by combining both the juice and pulp of lime or lemon, sugar (use agave nectar), fish sauce, fresh Thai chilies, and garlic, all crushed together in a mortar and pestle. This sauce is a perfect complement for steamed, boiled, or grilled seafood, including the tomalley of crab or lobster. Serve with a bowl of plain brown rice and stir-fried greens on the side for a complete, refreshing, and relatively light meal.

SPICY SHRIMP COCKTAIL

SERVES 6 | SERVING SIZE: 4 PIECES

Shrimp cocktail is easy to prepare, is refreshing, and should be served lightly chilled. Borrowed from the basic and popular American restaurant appetizer, this shrimp cocktail is served with a Asian-inspired dipping sauce that is spicy and savory at the same time with a hint of sweetness on the finish. You can also toss the shrimp with the chili-miso sauce and serve it over a bed of greens, turning an appetizer into a light lunch instantly.

24 peeled, headless, and deveined gulf shrimp

2 tablespoons shiro-miso

1/4 cup rice vinegar, or 3 tablespoons lemon juice

2 teaspoons dark sesame oil

1 teaspoon 100% pure maple syrup

1 teaspoon sriracha

1 Bring a medium pot of water to boil over high heat. Add the shrimp, and cook until opaque, 1–2 minutes. Drain and shock under cold running water. Drain again and refrigerate until ready to use.

2 Meanwhile, in a small bowl, whisk together the miso, rice vinegar, sesame oil, sriracha and maple syrup until well combined. Serve with chilled shrimp for dipping.

Calories 55
  Calories from Fat 20
Total Fat 2.0 g
  Saturated Fat 0.3 g
  Trans Fat 0.0 g
Cholesterol 45 mg

Sodium 180 mg
Potassium 60 mg
Total Carbohydrate 4 g
  Dietary Fiber 0 g
  Sugars 3 g
Protein 6 g

EXCHANGES/ CHOICES
1 Lean Meat

GRILLED SHRIMP WITH SOY GLAZE

SERVES 6 | SERVING SIZE: 4 PIECES

Shrimp seems to be a favorite protein for many. Quick to prepare, it takes on flavor easily and is ideal for all sorts of cooking techniques. Easy to handle, it makes for an ideal finger food at parties. Served hot, at room temperature, or lightly chilled, the glaze in this recipe gives a beautiful golden sheen to the shrimp for a beautiful presentation.

2 tablespoons light soy sauce

2 tablespoons sake

2 tablespoons rice vinegar

2 teaspoon dark sesame oil

1 teaspoon sriracha (optional)

1 large garlic clove, peeled and minced

1 scallion, trimmed and minced

1-inch piece ginger, peeled and minced

1 teaspoon agave nectar

1/2 teaspoon tapioca starch or cornstarch diluted with 1 tablespoon water

24 headless, peeled, deveined large tiger shrimp (about 2 pounds)

6 long bamboo skewers, soaked in water

1 Preheat grill to 500°F for 20 minutes.

2 Meanwhile, in a small pot, add the soy sauce, sake, vinegar, sesame oil, sriracha, garlic, scallion, ginger, and agave nectar over low heat until heated through. Continuously stirring, add the diluted tapioca starch, and continue to simmer until slightly thickened, about 30 seconds. Remove the glaze from the heat.

3 Thread 4 shrimp on each of the 6 skewers, and grill until opaque and golden, turning once, about 5 minutes total. Brush the shrimp with the glaze on both sides, and serve.

Calories 145	Sodium 470 mg
Calories from Fat 20	Potassium 265 mg
Total Fat 2.5 g	Total Carbohydrate 3 g
Saturated Fat 0.5 g	Dietary Fiber 0 g
Trans Fat 0.0 g	Sugars 1 g
Cholesterol 185 mg	Protein 25 g

EXCHANGES/ CHOICES
3 Lean Meat

MUSSELS IN SAKE SAUCE

SERVES 6 | SERVING SIZE: 2 CUPS

This recipe is a Japanese take on the French moules marinières, mussels cooked in white wine and butter sauce. All the ingredients are basic Asian aromatics—such as garlic, scallions, ginger, and cilantro with sake and coconut oil. Serve with brown sushi rice and a tossed salad with Lemon-Miso Dressing (page 9).

1 tablespoon grapeseed oil

4 large garlic cloves, peeled and crushed

4 scallions, trimmed and crushed

2-inch piece ginger, thinly sliced lengthwise

3 cups sake

1 teaspoon chili-garlic sauce (optional)

Low-sodium salt

Freshly ground black pepper

3 pounds mussels, soaked in water for 20 minutes, beards removed

1/2 bunch cilantro, stems trimmed

1. In a large pot, add the oil and stir-fry the garlic, scallions, and ginger over high heat until golden, 3 to 5 minutes. Add the sake and chili-garlic sauce (if using), and season with salt and pepper to taste.

2. Toss in the mussels, and scatter the cilantro on top. Place the lid on top, and cook until the mussels open, about 10 minutes. Serve hot.

Calories 310	**Sodium** 435 mg
Calories from Fat 70	**Potassium** 440 mg
Total Fat 8.0 g	**Total Carbohydrate** 15 g
Saturated Fat 1.2 g	**Dietary Fiber** 1 g
Trans Fat 0.0 g	**Sugars** 9 g
Cholesterol 65 mg	**Protein** 28 g

EXCHANGES/ CHOICES
1 Carbohydrate
4 Lean Meat
1/2 Fat
1/2 Alcohol

STIR-FRIED MIXED SEAFOOD WITH GINGER

SERVES 6 | SERVING SIZE: 1 1/2 CUPS

This stir-fry is a seafood lover's dream with scallops, squid, and shrimp thrown in the mix. Serve with noodles or rice and stir-fried vegetables. This is a meal that takes no more than 10 minutes to put on the table.

2 tablespoons grapeseed oil

2 large garlic cloves, peeled and thinly sliced

1 1/2-inch piece ginger, peeled and finely julienned

1 scallion, trimmed and chopped

1 jalapeño pepper, stem and seeds removed, pod thinly sliced

12 large shitake mushrooms, stems removed, caps quartered

3/4 pound bay scallops, drained and patted dry

1 pound headless, peeled, and deveined small shrimp, drained and patted dry

6 medium squids, cleaned, tentacles separated, bodies cut into 1/2-inch rings, drained, and patted dry

1 1/2 tablespoon light soy sauce

2 teaspoons dark sesame oil

Freshly ground black pepper

12 sprigs cilantro

1. In a large skillet over high heat, add the oil, and stir-fry the garlic, ginger, scallion, and jalapeño until fragrant and golden, 3 to 5 minutes.

2. Add the mushrooms, scallops, shrimp, and squids, and toss well to cook evenly throughout, about 10 minutes. Season with soy sauce, sesame oil, and black pepper, to taste. Transfer to a serving platter. Garnish with cilantro before serving hot.

Calories 175
Calories from Fat 115
Total Fat 13.0 g
Saturated Fat 2.0 g
Trans Fat 0.0 g
Cholesterol 15 mg

Sodium 160 mg
Potassium 370 mg
Total Carbohydrate 6 g
Dietary Fiber 4 g
Sugars 1 g
Protein 10 g

EXCHANGES/ CHOICES
1/2 Carbohydrate
1 Lean Meat
2 Fat

LOBSTER SALAD WITH GINGER, SCALLIONS, AND CILANTRO

SERVES 6 | SERVING SIZE: 1 CUP

Unlike the classic American lobster salad, this version contains no mayonnaise. Instead, it is tossed with creamy avocado in a miso sauce and served wrapped in lettuce, making for a healthful Asian-inspired version.

2 tablespoons rice vinegar

1 tablespoon shiro-miso

1 tablespoon dark sesame oil

1 tablespoon grapeseed oil

2 cooked lobsters, claw meat and tails, chopped (21 oz)

2 Haas avocados, halved, pitted, peeled, and chopped

1/2-ounce ginger, peeled and finely grated

1 scallion, trimmed and minced

1/3 cup cilantro leaves

Low-sodium salt

Freshly ground black pepper

1 Boston lettuce, leaves separated (12 medium to large leaves)

1 In a large bowl, stir together the vinegar, miso, and sesame and grapeseed oils. Toss in the lobster, avocados, ginger, scallions, and cilantro, and adjust seasoning with salt and pepper to taste. Serve with lettuce leaves on the side for wrapping.

Calories 250	**Sodium** 490 mg
Calories from Fat 135	**Potassium** 665 mg
Total Fat 15.0 g	**Total Carbohydrate** 8 g
Saturated Fat 2.0 g	**Dietary Fiber** 4 g
Trans Fat 0.0 g	**Sugars** 1 g
Cholesterol 70 mg	**Protein** 22 g

EXCHANGES/ CHOICES
1/2 Carbohydrate
3 Lean Meat
2 Fat

SPICY LIME-CURED BABY SCALLOPS AND SHRIMP WITH AVOCADO

SERVES 6 | SERVING SIZE: 1 CUP

This refreshing, citrusy Asian-inspired ceviche of scallops and shrimp will quickly become a favorite with guests. Easy to prepare, it requires quick poaching of the seafood and tossing in a lime-based dressing. Crunchy with cucumber and creamy with avocado, this seafood salad can be served as an appetizer or as a main entrée served over fresh baby greens.

1 pound bay scallops

1 pound headless, peeled, deveined rock shrimp

Juice of 2 limes (about 1/3 cup)

1 teaspoon dark sesame oil

1 tablespoon grapeseed oil

Low-sodium salt

Freshly ground black pepper

1 small tomato, finely chopped

1 small Haas avocado, peeled, pitted, and cubed

1 small Persian cucumber, finely diced

1/4 cup cilantro leaves

1 Bring a pot of water to boil over high heat. Add the scallops and shrimp, and cook for 30 seconds. Drain, shock in cold water, and drain again.

2 In a large bowl, stir together the lime juice and sesame and grapeseed oils, and season with salt and pepper to taste. Add the scallops, shrimp, tomato, avocado, cucumber, and cilantro leaves. Toss well. Serve in individual bowls or plates.

Calories 220	**Sodium** 240 mg	
Calories from Fat 80	**Potassium** 565 mg	
Total Fat 9.0 g	**Total Carbohydrate** 6 g	
Saturated Fat 1.2 g	**Dietary Fiber** 2 g	
Trans Fat 0.0 g	**Sugars** 1 g	
Cholesterol 140 mg	**Protein** 29 g	

EXCHANGES/ CHOICES
1/2 Carbohydrate
4 Lean Meat
1/2 Fat

SPICY SQUID SALAD WITH TAMARIND SAUCE

SERVES 6 | **SERVING SIZE: 1 CUP**

This Thai-inspired grilled squid salad is savory, tangy, sweet, spicy, and bitter all in the same bite. Refreshing, it is perfect for summer served with Basic Brown Rice ("Jasmine," page 61) and any kind of stir-fried greens on the side. The tamarind sauce is also wonderful with grilled shrimp or soft-shell crab.

12 squids, cleaned, tentacles separated

1 tablespoon grapeseed oil

Low-sodium salt

Freshly ground black pepper

1/4 cup tamarind concentrate or lime juice (about 1 lime)

2 tablespoons agave nectar

2 tablespoons fish sauce

1 medium garlic clove, peeled and minced

1/2 teaspoon chili-garlic sauce ("Sambal Olek")

1 small shallot, peeled and sliced into thin wedges

1 medium ripe tomato, sliced into thin wedges

6 sprigs Thai basil or cilantro, leaves only

1 Heat a well-oiled grill pan over high heat. Meanwhile, brush the squids with oil, and season lightly with salt and pepper. Grill the squids in batches, until golden, about 2 minutes per side. Slice the squids into 1-inch rings.

2 In the meantime, whisk together the tamarind concentrate, agave nectar, fish sauce, garlic, and chili-garlic sauce. Toss in the squids, shallots, and tomato and serve in individual bowls. Garnish each serving with basil or cilantro before serving.

Calories 165	**Sodium** 520 mg
Calories from Fat 35	**Potassium** 355 mg
Total Fat 4.0 g	**Total Carbohydrate** 11 g
Saturated Fat 0.7 g	**Dietary Fiber** 0 g
Trans Fat 0.0 g	**Sugars** 5 g
Cholesterol 300 mg	**Protein** 21 g

EXCHANGES/ CHOICES
1/2 Carbohydrate
3 Lean Meat

GRILLED SCALLOPS WITH BLACK BEAN SAUCE

SERVES 6 | **SERVING SIZE: 4 PIECES**

Black bean sauce is one of the most popular items on Chinese restaurant menus. Fermented black beans, which are oxidized soybeans, are found in Asian markets. Generally salted, they need to soak for 20 minutes before using in any recipe. Easy to make, Chinese black bean sauce requires a touch of ginger, garlic, and rice wine. That's all there is to it, and once made, the sauce can be used to enhance tofu, meats, or seafood.

2 tablespoons grapeseed oil, divided use

1 large garlic clove, peeled and minced

1-inch piece ginger, peeled and minced

1/3 cup Chinese black beans, soaked in water for 20 minutes, and drained

1 teaspoon chili-garlic sauce ("sambal olek," optional)

1/2 cup Chinese rice wine or Japanese sake

3 scallions, trimmed and cut into 1-inch pieces, the white parts halved lengthwise

24 large sea scallops

12 sprigs cilantro, stems trimmed

1 In a small skillet, add 1 tablespoon oil, and stir-fry the garlic and ginger over high heat until fragrant and golden, about 2 minutes. Add the black beans, chili-garlic sauce (if using), and wine. Reduce heat to low, and cook until some of the beans break down, about 10 minutes. Add the scallions, and continue to simmer until wilted, about 1 minute. Remove from heat.

2 In a large nonstick skillet, add the remaining oil, and wait until it starts to smoke. Add the scallops, and pan-fry until golden on both sides, about 3 minutes total. Transfer to a serving platter. Spoon the black bean sauce over each scallop, and garnish with cilantro.

Calories 150	**Sodium** 460 mg
Calories from Fat 55	**Potassium** 325 mg
Total Fat 6.0 g	**Total Carbohydrate** 7 g
Saturated Fat 0.7 g	**Dietary Fiber** 1 g
Trans Fat 0.0 g	**Sugars** 1 g
Cholesterol 25 mg	**Protein** 15 g

EXCHANGES/ CHOICES
1/2 Carbohydrate
2 Lean Meat
1/2 Fat

PAN-FRIED SEA BASS WITH SPICY PINEAPPLE CHUTNEY

SERVES 6 | SERVING SIZE: 1 FILET

Fresh fish and ripe pineapple are key to this dish. Chutneys are Indian condiments, similar to relish. This chutney relies on the natural sweetness and tanginess of the fruit itself. Sea bass, trout, tilapia, and other types of white fish pair well with this refreshing Indian-inspired pineapple chutney. Serve with salad and rice for a wholesome meal.

3 tablespoons grapeseed oil, divided use

2 large garlic cloves, peeled and minced

1 1/2-inch piece ginger, peeled and minced

1 medium red onion, peeled and minced

1 tablespoon Indian curry powder

1 small ripe pineapple, peeled, cored, and chopped

Juice and grated zest of 1 lemon (about 1/4 cup and 1 teaspoon, respectively)

Low-sodium salt

Freshly ground black pepper

2 1/2 pounds sea bass filets, skinless optional (6 individual filets)

1/3 cup rice flour

1 In a large skillet, add 1 tablespoon oil and sauté the garlic, ginger, and onion over medium heat until golden, 5 to 7 minutes. Add the curry powder, and continue to sauté until fragrant and a shade darker, about 2 minutes. Add the pineapple, and continue to cook until the natural juices have evaporated, and the pieces have broken down and turned golden, about 20 minutes. Add the lemon juice, and cook for 10 minutes more. Season with salt and pepper to taste, stir in the lemon zest, and remove from heat.

2 Meanwhile, season the filets lightly with salt and pepper on both sides, then dust each with flour. Shake the filets to get rid of excess flour. In a large nonstick skillet, add 1 tablespoon grapeseed oil, and pan-fry the filets over high heat, until golden on both sides and just flaky, about 5 minutes. Add the remaining oil, and pan-fry the rest of the filets. Drain on paper towels, and serve with some pineapple chutney on the side on or on top.

Calories 335	Sodium 135 mg
Calories from Fat 100	Potassium 665 mg
Total Fat 11.0 g	Total Carbohydrate 22 g
Saturated Fat 1.7 g	Dietary Fiber 2 g
Trans Fat 0.0 g	Sugars 9 g
Cholesterol 80 mg	Protein 36 g

EXCHANGES/ CHOICES
1/2 Starch
1/2 Fruit
1 Vegetable
5 Lean Meat

STEAMED STRIPED BASS WITH GINGER, SCALLIONS, AND SHITAKES

SERVES 6 | SERVING SIZE: 1/2 CUP

Steamed whole fish is popular in many parts of Asia. In Cantonese cooking, this classic recipe is made with either sea bass, flounder, or carp. Nothing could be simpler than making this steamed fish recipe. The most important part to this recipe is selecting the fish itself. Look for bright eyes, glossy skin, and a plump body that is firm to the touch. Serve with rice and a stir-fried leafy green vegetable.

2 1/2 pounds whole striped bass, cleaned (or two smaller fish)

1 1/2-inch piece ginger, peeled and finely julienned

6 medium to large dried shitakes, soaked in water until soft, stems removed, caps julienned

2 scallions, trimmed and cut into 1 1/2-inch long pieces, white parts halved lengthwise

1 1/2 tablespoons grapeseed oil

2 tablespoons light soy sauce

1 teaspoon dark sesame oil

6 sprigs cilantro

1 Place a rice bowl topped with an oval plate in the center of a wok. Fill with water to about 1 1/2 inches from the bottom of the plate.

2 Place the fish on top of the plate, garnish with ginger, shitakes, and scallions. Cover and bring to boil over high heat. Steam until the fish is cooked or just flaking, 15–20 minutes.

3 Carefully drain any liquid from the plate, and remove the plate from the wok. Pour the oil, soy sauce, and sesame oil over the fish while it is piping hot. Garnish with cilantro and serve hot.

Calories 130	**Sodium** 230 mg	**EXCHANGES/ CHOICES**
Calories from Fat 55	**Potassium** 270 mg	1/2 Carbohydrate
Total Fat 6.0 g	**Total Carbohydrate** 5 g	2 Lean Meat
Saturated Fat 0.8 g	**Dietary Fiber** 1 g	1/2 Fat
Trans Fat 0.0 g	**Sugars** 0 g	
Cholesterol 30 mg	**Protein** 15 g	

GRILLED SCALLOPS WITH BLACK BEAN SAUCE | page 102

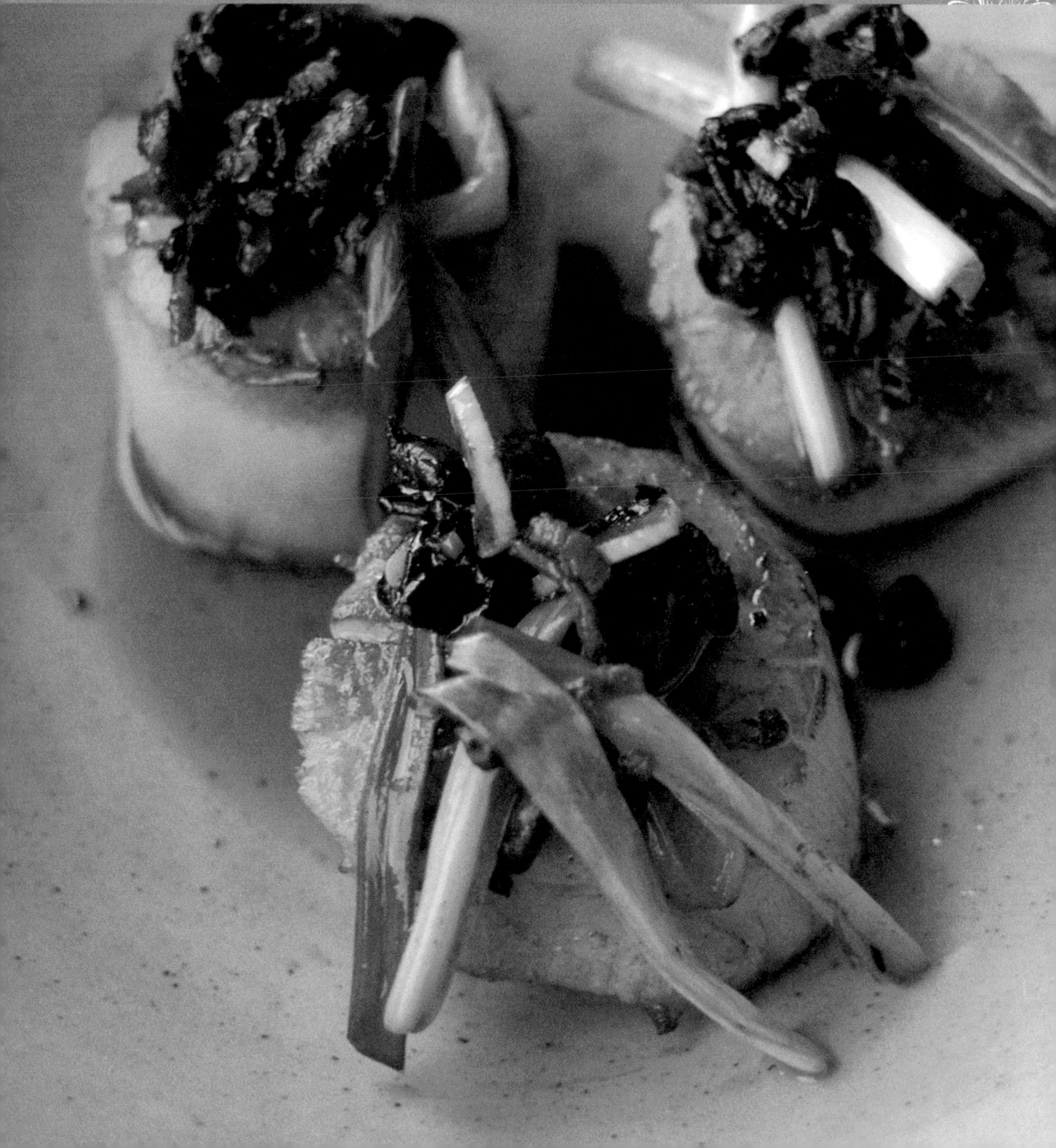

ABOVE: **FRESH VEGETABLE SUMMER ROLLS** | page 47
BELOW: **BAKED BANANA AND MANGO SPRING ROLLS** | page 130

CURRY-SPICED GRILLED SHRIMP

SERVES 6 | SERVING SIZE: 4 PIECES

Curry-Spiced Grilled Shrimp with a side of Poached Baby Bok Choy with Mushroom Sauce (page 79) over brown rice or buckwheat noodles makes for a delicious wholesome dinner. Served over a bed of fresh greens with Walnut-Miso Sauce (page 10), the shrimp are also perfect as a light lunch. Curry powder is an easy way to create flavor instantly. Sprinkle on seafood, meats, and vegetables, and transform a simple meal into something special for the family. *Tip: Grill, stir-fry, or pan-roast or broil.*

2 tablespoons grapeseed or vegetable oil

Juice of 1 lemon, and grated zest reserved separately

2 teaspoons curry powder

2 large garlic cloves, crushed, peeled, and minced

24 jumbo headless, peeled and deveined Tiger shrimp (about 2 1/2 lbs)

Low-sodium salt

Freshly ground black pepper

1 Preheat grill, broiler, or oven to 450°F for 20 minutes.

2 Meanwhile, in a large bowl, stir together the oil, lemon juice, curry, and garlic. Add the shrimp, season lightly with salt and pepper, mix well to coat evenly throughout, and marinate for 15 minutes.

3 Skewer the shrimp and grill, or scatter them on a cookie sheet and broil or roast them, until opaque and lightly golden, about 1 minute per side.

VARIATION

In a large skillet or wok, add the shrimp with marinade, and stir-fry over high heat until the shrimp turn opaque, about 3 minutes.

Calories 190	**Sodium** 210 mg
Calories from Fat 55	**Potassium** 305 mg
Total Fat 6.0 g	**Total Carbohydrate** 1 g
Saturated Fat 0.8 g	**Dietary Fiber** 0 g
Trans Fat 0.0 g	**Sugars** 0 g
Cholesterol 230 mg	**Protein** 31 g

EXCHANGES/ CHOICES
4 Lean Meat

SALMON TERIYAKI

SERVES 6 | SERVING SIZE: 1 FILET

This recipe is based on the popular Japanese restaurant special, oftentimes offering various options, including salmon, chicken, or tofu. Teriyaki is a sweet and savory soy sauce base that is used as a marinade and finishing sauce or glaze on the protein. Serve this simple and delightful dish with steamed vegetables over brown sushi rice for a classic bento box lunch special.

1/4 cup sake

1/4 cup light soy sauce

Juice of 1 lemon (about 1/4 cup)

1 tablespoon sesame oil

1 tablespoon agave nectar

1-inch piece ginger, thinly sliced

3 large garlic cloves, peeled

2 scallions, trimmed and knotted together or lightly crushed

Freshly crushed black pepper

1 teaspoon tapioca starch or cornstarch, diluted with 2 tablespoons water

2 tablespoons grapeseed oil

6 small salmon filets or steaks (about 2 pounds)

1 In a saucepan, add the sake, soy sauce, lemon juice, sesame oil, agave nectar, ginger, garlic, scallions, and pepper to taste. Simmer over low heat until heated through. Stir in the tapioca starch continuously until the sauce is slightly thickened. Remove sauce from the heat, and cool.

2 Use 2 tablespoons of the sauce to season the salmon filets or steaks, brushing the sauce all over each piece.

3 In a large nonstick skillet, add the oil. When the oil starts to smoke, add the filets or steaks, skin side down, and pan-fry over medium heat until golden, about 3 minutes. Flip and continue to pan-fry until just flaky, about 2 minutes. Remove from heat and serve hot, topped with remaining teriyaki sauce.

Calories 360	**Sodium** 450 mg
Calories from Fat 180	**Potassium** 520 mg
Total Fat 20.0 g	**Total Carbohydrate** 6 g
Saturated Fat 3.1 g	**Dietary Fiber** 0 g
Trans Fat 0.0 g	**Sugars** 3 g
Cholesterol 105 mg	**Protein** 35 g

EXCHANGES/ CHOICES .
1/2 Carbohydrate
5 Lean Meat
2 1/2 Fat

FRIED FISH WITH STIR-FRIED HERBS AND PEANUTS

SERVES 12 | SERVING SIZE: 1/2 CUP

A classic northern Vietnamese dish, this fried fish recipe is a crowd pleaser. Crunchy tender, sweet, savory, spicy, tangy, and bitter, it is typically served over rice vermicelli, though brown rice works well. A drizzle of the ubiquitous table condiment known as *nuoc cham* (Spicy Fish Sauce Dressing, page 12) completes the dish.

6 ounces rice vermicelli, soaked in cold water until pliable

2 cups grapeseed oil, plus 1 tablespoon, divided use

1 cup rice flour

1 teaspoon turmeric powder

1/2 teaspoon low-sodium salt

1/4 teaspoon ground black pepper

2 pounds of skinless catfish, flounder, or striped bass, cut into 1-inch pieces

1 bunch dill, stems trimmed

1 bunch Thai basil (leaves only), or cilantro, stems trimmed

1 cup unsalted roasted peanuts

Spicy Fish Sauce Dressing (page 12)

1 Bring a medium pot of water to a boil over high heat. Add the vermicelli, and cook until just tender, about 10 seconds. Drain and shock under cold running water. Drain and divide among 12 individual large soup plates or bowls.

2 Heat 2 cups oil in a small pot over medium-high heat. Meanwhile, in a resealable bag, add the flour, turmeric, salt, and pepper, and shake it to mix the ingredients thoroughly. Add the fish, and toss to coat well. Fry the fish in batches until golden and crispy, about 1 to 2 minutes. Drain on a paper towel, and divide among each serving of rice vermicelli.

3 In a large skillet, add the remaining tablespoon of oil, and stir-fry the dill and cilantro over high heat until wilted, about 1 minute. Add the peanuts, and continue to stir-fry for 1 minute more. Divide into 12 servings, and serve drizzled with Spicy Fish Sauce Dressing (page 12) to individual taste.

		EXCHANGES/ CHOICES
Calories 325	Sodium 125 mg	2 Starch
Calories from Fat 155	Potassium 440 mg	2 Lean Meat
Total Fat 17.0 g	Total Carbohydrate 26 g	2 Fat
Saturated Fat 2.5 g	Dietary Fiber 2 g	
Trans Fat 0.0 g	Sugars 1 g	
Cholesterol 45 mg	Protein 17 g	

CHAPTER SEVEN
Meat and Poultry

In Asia, meats and poultry are expensive when compared to the cost of seafood. For this reason, meat has always been enjoyed in small quantities. It is added to dishes mainly as a flavor enhancer. The only time meat is served in any great quantity is during holidays, birthdays, or special occasions. However, even then, a roasted bird or pan-fried steak is always shared amongst a full table of 6–8 persons. A few slices will go a long way!

Asian cultures have a "no waste" approach to cooking. Walk into a meat market in Chinatown, and you'll find pig intestines, bull's penis, duck tongues, and chicken feet, to name a few! None of these has been included here in this chapter; however, it is worth mentioning. To use an animal in its entirety is commendable. Protein fat replaces oil; duck wings and pork blood are preserved in salt, sugar, and spices and air dried; and more expensive parts, like pork tenderloin or chicken breast, are stir-fried, steamed, or poached.

Beef shin, oxtail, and short ribs are best braised or stewed over low heat for several hours until fork tender. Filet mignon, sirloin, and strip or hanger steak are best grilled and stir-fried.

Pork is the most widely eaten meat in Asia. It is also the least expensive. If you raise a pig, you're considered wealthy because you can feed many people with all the different parts of the pig. One pig or hog goes a long way.

Chicken and duck are also enjoyed, oftentimes during special holidays. Serving a chicken whole symbolizes unity, while duck symbolizes fidelity. It is no wonder then that these are often served during a wedding banquet. Today, these meats are enjoyed in any number of dishes throughout the year as well.

MEATY BONES FOR STOCK

It is always a good idea to reserve any meaty bones rather than waste them when prepping meat and poultry for cooking. Chicken backbones and wings, pork ribs, and oxtail are all perfect for making stocks. Just season lightly with fish sauce or salt, add crushed scallions and sliced ginger, and reduce the stock by half for several hours over low heat. Skim fat and strain, discarding any solids before storing the stock in quart containers. Stock will keep for up to 3 days refrigerated and 3 months in the freezer.

EVERYDAY EASY ASIAN MARINADE

A small quantity of marinade will go a long way. All you need is just enough to coat any meat or poultry. Anymore than that, and you are wasting good ingredients, drowning the meat unnecessarily! Meat does not absorb more flavor if you have more marinade than you need. It will absorb the flavor at the same rate, so be frugal and stir 1/4-cup light soy sauce, with 2 tablespoons agave nectar, 1 teaspoon chili-garlic paste (optional), 1 teaspoon five-spice powder (optional), 1 grated large garlic clove, 1 tablespoon grated fresh ginger, and 1 minced scallion. This amount is good for 1 to 2 pounds of meat. Marinate whole chickens or large cuts for 1 hour at room temperature or 2 hours refrigerated. If making satay (skewered meats), marinate for 30 minutes at room temperature.

FIVE-SPICE PAN-SEARED DUCK BREASTS

SERVES 6 | SERVING SIZE: 1/6 RECIPE

Chinese five-spice contains cassia, star anise, Sichuan peppercorns, cloves, and fennel seeds, though slight variations exist. This powder mixed with either fish sauce or soy sauce, a small amount of sweetener to counterbalance the salt, and any number of herbs makes for a delicious marinade that can be used on any meat protein, including duck. Duck breasts tend to be large, weighing 10 ounces on average.

1/3 cup light soy sauce or fish sauce

1 tablespoon agave nectar

1 large garlic clove, peeled and grated

1-inch piece ginger, peeled and grated

1 scallion, trimmed and minced

1 teaspoon Chinese five-spice powder (page 6)

2 pounds duck breasts (3 large duck breasts), skin and fat removed

2 tablespoons oil (use only if discarding skin from duck breasts)

1 In a gallon-sized resealable plastic bag, add the soy sauce, agave nectar, garlic, ginger, scallion, and five-spice powder (page 6). Mix well. Add the duck breasts, coat them evenly, and press the bag while sealing to remove excess air. Let marinate for 20 minutes.

2 Heat a large skillet and add the duck breasts skin side down. Cook over medium heat until the skin is golden crisp and the fat has rendered, about 3 minutes. Flip and cook for 4 to 5 minutes more, or until desired doneness. (**Note:** If using skinless duck breasts, heat the oil in the skillet, and proceed with step 2.)

Calories 200
Calories from Fat 65
Total Fat 7.0 g
Saturated Fat 0.9 g
Trans Fat 0.0 g
Cholesterol 135 mg

Sodium 585 mg
Potassium 308 mg
Total Carbohydrate 5 g
Dietary Fiber 0 g
Sugars 2 g
Protein 28 g

EXCHANGES/ CHOICES
1/2 Carbohydrate
4 Lean Meat

BRAISED DUCK IN SPICY ORANGE-LEMONGRASS SAUCE

SERVES 6 | **SERVING SIZE: 1/2 CUP**

Braising is a wonderful cooking technique, especially during the fall and winter, when we need to warm up. Slow-cooked over low heat, the duck—in its Vietnamese-French-inspired orange sauce—becomes very tender and falls off the bones. Serve with Basic Brown Rice ("Jasmine," page 61) and any stir-fried leafy greens.

1 4-pound duck, skin and fat removed

1 head garlic, cloves peeled

1 medium onion, peeled

6 cloves

1 quart freshly squeezed orange juice (about 8 oranges)

3 cups Asian Chicken Stock (page 17)

2 tablespoons fish sauce

1 4-inch long cinnamon stick

6 pieces star anise

3 whole red Thai chilies, or 3 dried red chilies

3 scallions, trimmed, twisted, and knotted together (or separately

3 stalks lemongrass, trimmed, twisted, and knotted together (or separately)

1 In a large, heavy-bottomed pot, brown the duck on all sides over medium heat until the skin is golden brown, about 20 minutes. Remove the duck from pot, and add the garlic, onion, and cloves, and cook until fragrant and golden, about 3 minutes.

2 Place the duck back into the pot, along with the orange juice, stock, fish sauce, cinnamon, star anise, chilies, scallions, and lemongrass. Lower the heat to medium-low, cover with lid, and cook until the duck meat falls off the bones and the sauce is reduced by at least half, about 4 hours. Skim the fat off the top and discard, and serve duck with sauce on the side.

VARIATION

Preheat oven to 325°F, and braise for 4 hours.

Calories 225
  Calories from Fat 70
Total Fat 8.0 g
  Saturated Fat 2.7 g
  Trans Fat 0.0 g
Cholesterol 60 mg

Sodium 560 mg
Potassium 545 mg
Total Carbohydrate 19 g
  Dietary Fiber 0 g
  Sugars 14 g
Protein 18 g

EXCHANGES/ CHOICES
1 Fruit
3 Lean Meat
1/2 Fat

FIVE-SPICE RACK OF LAMB

SERVES 6 | SERVING SIZE: 3 PIECES

Rack of lamb is as perfect for the grill during the summer, as it is for the oven during the cooler months of the year. Here, a classic marinade using Chinese Five-Spice Powder (page 6) sweetens otherwise pungent meat. Relatively small in size, a rack of lamb will serve two. Be sure to remove most of the fat when trimming, but leave a little fat on it. It is the fat mixed with this complex spice blend that will deepen the flavor of the meat as it melts and crisps. If you don't like trimming yourself, ask the butcher to "French" the rack, removing the fat among the bones.

1/3 cup light soy sauce or fish sauce

1 tablespoon agave nectar

1 large garlic clove, peeled and grated

1-inch piece ginger, peeled and grated

1 scallion, trimmed and minced

1 teaspoon Chinese five-spice powder (page 6)

2 1/2 pounds (3 racks) lamb, Frenched

1 Preheat the oven to 400°F. In a gallon-sized resealable plastic bag, add the soy sauce, agave nectar, garlic, ginger, scallion, and five-spice powder (page 6). Mix well. Add the lamb, coat the racks evenly, and press the bag while sealing to remove excess air. Let marinate for 20 minutes.

2 Place the racks on a roasting pan, and place in the oven. Roast until golden brown and medium rare, about 20 minutes, or desired doneness.

		EXCHANGES/ CHOICES
Calories 180	Sodium 540 mg	1/2 Carbohydrate
Calories from Fat 80	Potassium 260 mg	3 Lean Meat
Total Fat 9.0 g	Total Carbohydrate 5 g	1/2 Fat
Saturated Fat 3.2 g	Dietary Fiber 0 g	
Trans Fat 0.0 g	Sugars 2 g	
Cholesterol 60 mg	Protein 19 g	

POMEGRANATE-GINGER LEG OF LAMB

SERVES 12 | SERVING SIZE: 1/2 CUP

This pomegranate-ginger infused leg of lamb is braised until the meat shreds and mixes with its own juices. A perfect winter dish, this slow-cooked meal is even better when reheated. Serve with Basic Brown Rice ("Basmati," page 61) and grilled vegetables. *Note: This is a perfect dish to make if you want leftovers or are having a dinner party. Calculate about 3 to 5 ounces per serving.*

1/3 cup pomegranate extract or concentrate

2-ounces ginger, peeled and finely grated

4 garlic cloves, peeled and finely grated

1 shallot, peeled and finely grated

1 bunch cilantro, stems trimmed, and minced

1 small boneless leg of lamb (about 7 pounds), butterflied

Low-sodium salt

Freshly ground black pepper

2 tablespoons grapeseed oil

8 scallions, trimmed, crushed

1 In a large bowl, mix together the pomegranate, ginger, garlic, shallot, and cilantro.

2 Place the butterflied leg of lamb flat on a baking sheet. Salt and pepper across the top, and spread the pomegranate mixture all over. Roll up the meat, and tie with kitchen string several times around. Season with salt and pepper on the outside.

3 In a medium, heavy-bottomed pot, add the oil, and brown the lamb over medium-high heat on all sides, about 20 minutes. Add water halfway up the meat, add the scallions, and bring to a boil. Reduce heat to medium-low, and cook, covered, until the lamb is fork tender, about 5 hours. Skim off any fat, and serve hot.

VARIATION

Preheat oven to 325°F, cover, and braise lamb for 5 hours.

Calories 325
Calories from Fat 135
Total Fat 15.0 g
Saturated Fat 5.0 g
Trans Fat 0.0 g
Cholesterol 125 mg

Sodium 90 mg
Potassium 635 mg
Total Carbohydrate 6 g
Dietary Fiber 1 g
Sugars 4 g
Protein 38 g

EXCHANGES/ CHOICES
1/2 Carbohydrate
5 Lean Meat
1 1/2 Fat

BRAISED LAMB SHANKS IN SPICY GINGER-CHILI SAUCE

SERVES 6 | SERVING SIZE: 1/2 CUP

Braised or stewed dishes are especially welcomed during the colder months of the year, when the kitchen tends to warm the rest of the house and fill it with sweet aromas. This ginger- and chili-spiced lamb is absolutely delicious, especially sweetened with carrots and shallots and infused with refreshing cilantro.

2 tablespoons grapeseed oil

6 lamb shanks (about 3/4 lb each)

1 head garlic, cloves crushed and peeled

18 small shallots, peeled

2-ounces ginger, peeled and thinly sliced lengthwise

4 cups sake

1/4 cup light soy sauce

3 or more whole red Thai chilies, or 3 dried red chilies

6 large carrots, peeled and cut into 1-inch pieces

1 bunch cilantro, stems trimmed

2 cups water

1. In a large, heavy-bottomed pot, add the oil, and brown the lamb shanks over medium heat, about 20 minutes total. Remove the shanks from the pot. Add the garlic, shallots, and ginger and cook until fragrant and golden, about 5 to 7 minutes.

2. Return the shanks to the pot along with the sake, soy sauce, chilies, carrots, cilantro, and water, and cook partially covered for 4 hours. Skim the fat off the top, and serve hot.

Calories 300	**Sodium** 500 mg
Calories from Fat 100	**Potassium** 750 mg
Total Fat 11.0 g	**Total Carbohydrate** 17 g
Saturated Fat 2.6 g	**Dietary Fiber** 4 g
Trans Fat 0.0 g	**Sugars** 5 g
Cholesterol 100 mg	**Protein** 33 g

EXCHANGES/ CHOICES
3 Vegetable
4 Lean Meat
1 Fat

SWEET AND SPICY BRAISED BEEF WITH CARROTS

SERVES 6 | **SERVING SIZE: 1/2 CUP**

This Colonial French-Vietnamese-inspired dish, is derived from a French classic called *boeuf aux carottes*. It is served over rice with stir-fried greens on the side for a balanced meal during the coolest months of the year. Short ribs, oxtail, and shin are perfect for slow-cooking—the meats breaking down until tender without drying.

2 tablespoons grapeseed oil (skip if using short ribs or oxtail)

4 pounds beef shank, cut into 2-inch cubes

1 head garlic

12 small shallots, peeled

2 ounces ginger, thinly sliced lengthwise

2 teaspoons Chinese five-spice powder (page 6)

1/4 cup fish sauce

3 stalks lemongrass, trimmed, twisted and knotted together or separately

12 large carrots, cut into 1-inch thick pieces

Freshly ground black pepper

1. In a large heavy-bottomed pot, add the oil, and brown the meat on all sides over medium-high heat, about 20 minutes. Remove the meat from the pot, and add the garlic, shallots, and ginger, and stir-fry until fragrant and golden, about 5 minutes.

2. Return the meat to the pot, and add water halfway up the meat. Add the five-spice powder, fish sauce, and lemongrass, and bring to a boil. Reduce heat to medium-low and cook, covered, for 3 1/2 hours. Add the carrots, and continue to cook, covered, until the meat is fork tender, about 1 hour more. Season with freshly ground black pepper to taste.

Calories 375	**Sodium** 1085 mg	**EXCHANGES/ CHOICES**
Calories from Fat 110	**Potassium** 1190 mg	4 Vegetable
Total Fat 12.0 g	**Total Carbohydrate** 24 g	5 Lean Meat
Saturated Fat 3.1 g	**Dietary Fiber** 6 g	1 Fat
Trans Fat 0.0 g	**Sugars** 9 g	
Cholesterol 90 mg	**Protein** 42 g	

MISO-MARINATED BEEF TENDERLOIN

SERVES 6 | SERVING SIZE: 1/2 CUP

This is one of the easiest recipes for marinating beef tenderloin—it requires only 4 ingredients. It uses red miso, which is a salty soybean paste that is actually brown in color. Tenderloin is a very tender cut of meat that is lean and can absorb flavors easily. Wiped clean, you can grill or pan-sear the tenderloin. Thinly slice and serve atop salad greens for a relatively light meal.

1/3 cup aka-miso (red miso) paste
2 1/2 pounds beef tenderloin
2 tablespoons grapeseed oil
Freshly ground black pepper

1 Rub the miso paste all over each piece of beef tenderloin. Place in a resealable plastic bag, and seal while squeezing out any air. Let marinate for 1 hour at room temperature.

2 Meanwhile, preheat grill to medium-high heat for 20 minutes, if grilling. (If pan-searing, heat pan over medium-high heat, add the oil, and cook the tenderloin until medium-rare, about 5 minutes, or longer for desired doneness.)

3 Wipe the beef tenderloin clean, and discard the miso. Add the pieces, and cook until golden on the outside and medium-rare on the inside, flipping once, about 7 minutes total, or longer to desired doneness.

Calories 290	**Sodium** 330 mg
Calories from Fat 135	**Potassium** 455 mg
Total Fat 15.0 g	**Total Carbohydrate** 2 g
Saturated Fat 4.2 g	**Dietary Fiber** 0 g
Trans Fat 0.0 g	**Sugars** 0 g
Cholesterol 100 mg	**Protein** 36 g

EXCHANGES/ CHOICES
5 Lean Meat
1 1/2 Fat

BEEF TERIYAKI

SERVES 6 | **SERVING SIZE: 1/2 CUP**

This Japanese-inspired teriyaki is sure to be one of your go-to classics. Versatile, the sauce pairs well with any protein, including beef. Spinach makes for a wonderful side dish but can also be incorporated to create a nice appetizer. Slice the beef thinly, and roll up each slice with a spoonful of chopped sautéed spinach inside. This easy dish makes a beautiful presentation.

1/4 cup sake

1/4 cup light soy sauce

Juice of 1 lemon (about 1/4 cup)

1 tablespoon sesame oil

1 tablespoon agave nectar

1-inch piece ginger, thinly sliced

3 large garlic cloves, peeled

2 scallions, trimmed and knotted together or lightly crushed

Freshly crushed black pepper

1 teaspoon tapioca starch or cornstarch, diluted with 2 tablespoons water

2 tablespoons grapeseed oil

2 pounds flank steak (often labeled "London broil")

1 In a saucepan, add the sake, soy sauce, lemon juice, sesame oil, agave nectar, ginger, garlic, scallions, and pepper, and cook over low heat. Simmer until heated through. Stir in the tapioca starch continuously until the sauce is slightly thickened. Remove sauce from the heat, and cool.

2 Use 2 tablespoons of the sauce to season the steak.

3 Add the oil to a large nonstick skillet. When it starts to smoke, add the steak, and pan-fry over medium heat, until golden, about 5 minutes per side. Remove from heat, and serve hot, topped with remaining teriyaki sauce.

Calories 295	**Sodium** 435 mg
Calories from Fat 135	**Potassium** 445 mg
Total Fat 15.0 g	**Total Carbohydrate** 6 g
Saturated Fat 4.0 g	**Dietary Fiber** 0 g
Trans Fat 0.0 g	**Sugars** 3 g
Cholesterol 50 mg	**Protein** 31 g

EXCHANGES/ CHOICES
1/2 Carbohydrate
4 Lean Meat
1 1/2 Fat

BRAISED SPICY TURKEY AND TOFU STEW

SERVES 6 | SERVING SIZE: 1/2 CUP

This ground turkey and tofu dish is based on the classic Chinese Szechuan dish called ma po do fu, though the original uses pork. This healthier version is loaded with garlic, ginger, and scallions, three very important ingredient combinations in Chinese cooking. Like any braised or stewed dish, this one is even better reheated the next day. Serve over rice with stir-fried greens on the side.

1 tablespoon grapeseed oil

3 large garlic cloves, peeled and minced

1 1/2-ounces ginger, peeled and minced

2 scallions, trimmed and minced

1 pound lean ground turkey (93% lean)

2 pounds firm tofu, drained and cubed

2 tablespoons light soy sauce

1 cup Chinese rice wine or sake

1 cup water

1 tablespoon dark sesame oil

12 sprigs cilantro

1   In a medium, heavy-bottomed pot, add the oil, and stir-fry the garlic, ginger, and scallions, over high heat, until fragrant and golden, about 3 minutes. Add the ground turkey, and continue to cook until lightly browned, about 5 minutes more.

2   Add the tofu, soy sauce, wine, water, and sesame oil. Reduce the heat to low and cook, covered, until the tofu breaks apart, about 20 minutes. Garnish with cilantro, and serve hot.

Calories 290	**Sodium** 260 mg	**EXCHANGES/ CHOICES**
Calories from Fat 155	**Potassium** 470 mg	1/2 Carbohydrate
Total Fat 17.0 g	**Total Carbohydrate** 6 g	4 Lean Meat
Saturated Fat 3.5 g	**Dietary Fiber** 2 g	2 Fat
Trans Fat 0.1 g	**Sugars** 1 g	
Cholesterol 55 mg	**Protein** 27 g	

GRILLED LEMONGRASS PORK CHOPS

SERVES 6 | SERVING SIZE: 1 PIECE

Widely used in Southeast Asia, lemongrass gives a refreshing lemon-like flavor to any dish, but without the sharp citrusy note. Ground and mixed with garlic, fish sauce, and a natural sweetener, it becomes one of the most basic and classic marinades used on any number of seafood and/or meat proteins throughout Southeast Asia.

Note: Lemongrass is a very fibrous plant and can be prepped for cooking in any number of ways. When used in marinades, it is essential to break down the very coarse fiber by grating it finely, to make it easily digestible.

1 stalk lemongrass, trimmed and finely ground

2 garlic cloves, trimmed and finely grated

1 tablespoon fish sauce

1 tablespoon agave nectar

1 red Thai chili, stems and seeds removed, pod minced (optional)

1 tablespoon grapeseed oil

2 1/2 pounds pork chops (6 pieces total)

1 Preheat the grill to medium for 20 minutes. Meanwhile, mix together the lemongrass, garlic, fish sauce, agave nectar, chili (if using), and oil in a bowl.

2 Rub the herbal paste all over each pork chop, and grill until golden on both sides and cooked to medium, about 7 minutes (or desired doneness).

Calories 220	Sodium 285 mg	**EXCHANGES/ CHOICES**
Calories from Fat 90	Potassium 380 mg	4 Lean Meat
Total Fat 10.0 g	Total Carbohydrate 3 g	1 Fat
Saturated Fat 3.1 g	Dietary Fiber 0 g	
Trans Fat 0.0 g	Sugars 2 g	
Cholesterol 80 mg	Protein 28 g	

SPICY GROUND PORK LETTUCE WRAPS

SERVES 6 | SERVING SIZE: 1/2 CUP

Moo shoo pork is a popular menu item in Chinese restaurants. It is stir-fried ground pork served wrapped up in crunchy lettuce leaves. This dish is also delicious made with chicken or shrimp. It's a perfect-sized dish to serve as an appetizer or light meal.

1 tablespoon grapeseed oil

1 large garlic clove, peeled and minced

1-inch ginger, peeled and minced

2 scallions, trimmed and thinly sliced

2 pounds ground pork (96% lean)

1 tablespoon sesame oil

1 tablespoon light soy sauce

2 teaspoons Hoisin sauce

1 teaspoon chili-garlic sauce

1 head Boston lettuce, leaves separated, ribs trimmed

1 In a large skillet, add the oil and stir-fry the garlic, ginger, and scallions, over medium heat until fragrant. Add the pork, and continue to stir-fry, breaking it down and cooking it through, about 5 minutes.

2 Add the sesame oil, soy sauce, Hoisin sauce, and chili-garlic sauce (if using), and continue to stir until well combined. Remove from heat, and serve with lettuce leaves on the side for wrapping.

Calories 245	Sodium 220 mg
Calories from Fat 110	Potassium 515 mg
Total Fat 12.0 g	Total Carbohydrate 3 g
Saturated Fat 2.6 g	Dietary Fiber 0 g
Trans Fat 0.0 g	Sugars 1 g
Cholesterol 80 mg	Protein 32 g

EXCHANGES/ CHOICES
5 Lean Meat
1/2 Fat

CHICKEN CURRY WITH BROCCOLI AND MUSHROOMS

SERVES 6 | SERVING SIZE: 1 1/2 CUPS

Curry is eaten all over the world, but the most popular versions originate in India and Thailand. The Japanese have a mild version that uses Indian curry powder and stock as a base. A balanced meal in itself, it can be served as is or over Basic Brown Rice ("Sushi," page 61).

2 tablespoons grapeseed oil

1 small onion, sliced into thin wedges

1 tablespoon curry powder

1 quart Asian Chicken Stock (page 17)

1 tablespoon light soy sauce

1 ounce ginger, thinly sliced lengthwise

1 large carrot, cubed

10 white or brown cap mushrooms, stems trimmed, caps quartered

1 large waxy potato, peeled and cubed

1 pound skinless, boneless chicken breasts or thighs (about 3 pieces)

3 cups broccoli florets (about 1 large stalk)

2 teaspoons tapioca starch or cornstarch diluted in 2 tablespoons water

Low-sodium salt

Freshly ground black pepper

1. In a large, heavy-bottom pot, add the oil, and sauté the onion over medium heat until golden, about 5 minutes. Add the curry powder, and stir well, until fragrant, about 30 seconds. Add the stock, soy sauce, ginger, carrot, mushrooms, potato, and chicken, and cook until tender, about 25 minutes. Add the broccoli and cook for 5 minutes more.

2. Stir in the tapioca starch until the sauce is thickened, about 1 minute. Adjust the seasoning with salt and pepper, and serve hot over rice.

Calories 195	**Sodium** 235 mg	
Calories from Fat 65	**Potassium** 540 mg	
Total Fat 7.0 g	**Total Carbohydrate** 14 g	
Saturated Fat 1.1 g	**Dietary Fiber** 3 g	
Trans Fat 0.0 g	**Sugars** 3 g	
Cholesterol 45 mg	**Protein** 20 g	

EXCHANGES/ CHOICES
1/2 Starch
1 Vegetable
2 Lean Meat
1 Fat

BRAISED SOY SAUCE CHICKEN

SERVES 6 | **SERVING SIZE: 1/2 CUP**

This recipe is influenced by the Chinatown Cantonese restaurant chicken specialty. Cooked, soy glazed birds are often displayed in the front windows to entice potential customers. Cooked whole in a heavy Dutch oven, the chicken is cooled and carved in multiple pieces.

1 whole 3-pound chicken, skin removed

2 ounces ginger, thinly sliced

6 ounces scallions, lightly crushed

6 large garlic cloves, peeled

1/4 cup light soy sauce

2 tablespoons agave nectar

2 to 3 whole dried red chilies

6 sprigs cilantro

1 In a large, heavy-bottomed pot, add the chicken stuffed with the ginger, scallions, and garlic. Add water halfway up the chicken. Add soy sauce, agave nectar, and chilies. Bring to a boil over high heat.

2 Reduce heat to medium-low, and braise until the chicken is cooked through, about 1 1/2 hours. Remove the chicken from the pot, and reduce the sauce to half. Stir in the tapioca starch until the sauce thickens. Brush the sauce on the chicken, reserving the rest of it.

3 Once cooled, split the chicken into breast, wings, and legs. Cut the breast into 12 pieces, and the legs into 8 pieces. Arrange the pieces on a plate, and garnish with cilantro. Serve the remaining sauce on the side, for dipping.

Calories 210
  Calories from Fat 70
Total Fat 8.0 g
  Saturated Fat 2.2 g
  Trans Fat 0.0 g
Cholesterol 55 mg

Sodium 430 mg
Potassium 300 mg
Total Carbohydrate 10 g
  Dietary Fiber 1 g
  Sugars 5 g
Protein 23 g

EXCHANGES/ CHOICES
1/2 Carbohydrate
3 Lean Meat

SALT-BAKED CHICKEN WITH GINGER-SCALLION SAUCE

SERVES 6 | **SERVING SIZE: 1/2 CUP**

Salt-baked chicken is very simple and requires very few ingredients. The chicken is not as overly salty as one might think—the salt is only used as a baking vessel for the chicken. For this dish, low-sodium salt will do.

2 pounds low-sodium salt

1 large piece parchment paper

1 3-pound chicken (no skin)

4 scallions, trimmed and crushed

2 ounces ginger, thinly sliced lengthwise

6 garlic cloves, peeled and crushed

1 Preheat the oven to 375°F.

2 In a medium, heavy-bottomed clay pot, add 4 cups salt. Flatten the parchment paper on your work surface, place the chicken on top, and fill the cavity of the chicken with scallions, ginger, and cloves.

3 Wrap the chicken with the parchment, making sure it is completely enclosed, and place it on top of the salt. Fill the pot with the remaining salt, making sure the chicken is completely covered.

4 Bake until the juices run clear, about 2 hours. Let chicken rest for 15 minutes, then remove and discard skin before carving.

Calories 175	Sodium 55 mg
Calories from Fat 70	Potassium 215 mg
Total Fat 8.0 g	Total Carbohydrate 3 g
Saturated Fat 2.1 g	Dietary Fiber 0 g
Trans Fat 0.0 g	Sugars 0 g
Cholesterol 55 mg	Protein 21 g

EXCHANGES/ CHOICES
3 Lean Meat
1 Fat

GRILLED LEMONGRASS CHICKEN THIGHS

SERVES 6 | SERVING SIZE: 1 PIECE

A Vietnamese-inspired favorite, grilled lemongrass-infused chicken thighs are often served over rice with raw vegetables, including shredded or torn tender lettuce leaves, sliced cucumbers, julienned carrots, and fresh mint leaves. Drizzled with the ubiquitous Spicy Fish Sauce Dressing (page 12), it makes for a refreshing and relatively light meal, perfect for hot summer days.

1 stalk lemongrass, trimmed and finely ground

2 garlic cloves, trimmed and finely grated

2 tablespoons fish sauce

2 tablespoons agave nectar

1 red Thai chili, stems and seeds removed, pod minced (optional)

1 tablespoon grapeseed oil

2 1/2 pounds skinless chicken thighs (6 pieces total)

1 Preheat the grill to medium for 20 minutes.

2 Meanwhile, in a bowl, mix together the lemongrass, garlic, fish sauce, agave nectar, chili (if using), and oil.

3 Rub the herbal paste all over each chicken thigh, and grill until golden on both sides and cooked to medium (or desired doneness), about 15 minutes.

Calories 235	Sodium 540 mg	**EXCHANGES/ CHOICES**
Calories from Fat 110	Potassium 270 mg	1/2 Carbohydrate
Total Fat 12.0 g	Total Carbohydrate 5 g	3 Lean Meat
Saturated Fat 3.1 g	Dietary Fiber 0 g	1 1/2 Fat
Trans Fat 0.0 g	Sugars 4 g	
Cholesterol 90 mg	Protein 25 g	

GRILLED SPICY SOY SAUCE CHICKEN LEGS

SERVES 6 | **SERVING SIZE: 1/2 LEG OR BREAST**

This classic soy sauce-marinated chicken is full of delicious herbal notes from garlic, scallions, ginger, and cilantro. Sweetened with coconut palm sugar, the flavors are perfectly balanced and subtle. Serve with rice and salad on the side.

1/4 cup light soy sauce

2 tablespoons palm sugar or agave nectar

2 tablespoons grapeseed or vegetable oil

1 tablespoon sesame oil

2 teaspoons chili-garlic sauce (sambal olek or sriracha)

1 large garlic clove, crushed, peeled, and minced

1 ounce ginger, peeled and finely grated

1 scallion, trimmed and minced

4 small chicken legs or breasts, skinless and boneless

1. In a large bowl, whisk together the soy sauce and sugar until the sugar is completely dissolved. Stir in the grapeseed and sesame oils, chili-garlic sauce, garlic, ginger, and scallion. Pour into a large sealable gallon-sized plastic bag, and add the chicken pieces. Squeeze any air out of the bag, seal, and marinate refrigerated for 2 hours.

2. Preheat the grill to medium, or the oven to 425°F for 20 minutes. Place the chicken directly on the grill or in a roasting pan, and cook until the juices run clear, about 25 minutes.

Calories 215	**Sodium** 460 mg
Calories from Fat 110	**Potassium** 200 mg
Total Fat 12.0 g	**Total Carbohydrate** 7 g
Saturated Fat 2.2 g	**Dietary Fiber** 0 g
Trans Fat 0.0 g	**Sugars** 5 g
Cholesterol 60 mg	**Protein** 18 g

EXCHANGES/ CHOICES
1/2 Carbohydrate
3 Lean Meat
1 Fat

CHICKEN TERIYAKI

SERVES 6 | SERVING SIZE: 1/2 CUP

"Teriyaki" means grilled chicken in Japanese. Of all the teriyaki dishes on the Japanese menu, chicken is the most popular one. In Japan, the chicken is skewered, brushed with teriyaki sauce, and grilled and served as an hors d'oeuvre. *Note: You can turn any seafood or meat teriyaki into skewered and grilled small bites, which are perfect for parties.*

1/4 cup sake

1/4 cup light soy sauce

Juice of 1 lemon (about 1/4 cup)

1 tablespoon sesame oil

1 tablespoon agave nectar

1-inch piece ginger, thinly sliced

3 large garlic cloves, peeled

2 scallions, trimmed and knotted together, or lightly crushed

Freshly crushed black pepper

1 teaspoon tapioca starch or cornstarch, diluted with 2 tablespoons water

2 pounds skinless, boneless chicken thighs or breasts, cut into 1-inch cubes

2 tablespoons grapeseed oil

1 In a saucepan, add the sake, soy sauce, lemon juice, sesame oil, agave nectar, ginger, garlic, scallions, and pepper, and cook over low heat. Simmer until heated through. Stir in the tapioca starch continuously until the sauce is slightly thickened. Remove sauce from the heat, and allow it to cool.

2 Season the chicken with 2 tablespoons of the cooled sauce.

3 In a large nonstick skillet, heat the oil over medium heat. When the oil starts to smoke, add the chicken, and pan-fry until golden, about 5 minutes per side. Remove from heat and serve hot, topped with remaining teriyaki sauce.

Calories 250	**Sodium** 440 mg	**EXCHANGES/ CHOICES**
Calories from Fat 135	**Potassium** 250 mg	1/2 Carbohydrate
Total Fat 15.0 g	**Total Carbohydrate** 6 g	3 Lean Meat
Saturated Fat 3.0 g	**Dietary Fiber** 0 g	2 Fat
Trans Fat 0.0 g	**Sugars** 3 g	
Cholesterol 70 mg	**Protein** 21 g	

CHAPTER EIGHT
Sweets

Asian meals are balanced and created around the idea that all five flavor notes—sweet, sour, salty, spicy, and bitter—are present either in a single dish or distributed over several dishes in a single meal. For this reason, desserts are not traditionally served. Fresh fruit, especially oranges, are served at the end of the meal to help with digestion.

In Asia, "desserts," or at least what we think of as desserts, are enjoyed as afternoon snacks or during special celebrations such as weddings or birthdays. In essence, sweet foods are thought of as "sometimes foods" and are enjoyed with tea.

It's worth mentioning that tea is generally taken unsweetened, for the simple reason that foods generally have a sweet element, especially snacks. Tea is meant to help digest and dilute these sweet notes.

CLASSIC COCONUT TAPIOCA SOUP FOR ALL SEASONS

One classic dessert, which requires only a handful of ingredients, is coconut tapioca soup. This soup is enjoyed in China, Vietnam, Cambodia, Laos, and Thailand. It can be eaten piping hot, chilled, or at room temperature, depending on the season or your mood. You can add chopped bananas, mango, cooked and diced taro or sweet potato, and fresh corn off the cob in the summer.

Bring a pot filled with 1 1/2 quarts unsweetened, low-fat coconut milk to a gentle boil over medium heat. Add 2 tablespoons agave nectar, 1/2 teaspoon low-sodium salt, and a lemongrass stalk, trimmed and knotted (optional). Add 1/3 cup tapioca pearls and stir continuously so they do not clump, and cook until they are fully transparent, about 30 minutes. At this point, you can add any combination of banana, corn, or mango, or all three. You get the idea. The possibilities are endless. A sprinkle of toasted sesame seeds adds texture, flavor, and color and will complete this delightful, lightly sweetened dessert. A half a cup is the perfect serving size.

BAKED BANANA AND MANGO SPRING ROLLS

SERVES 6 | SERVING SIZE: 1 ROLL

Naturally, fruit-sweetened spring rolls are great for dessert or served as a snack in the afternoon. Filled with banana and mango, these spring rolls are inspired by a similar Filipino dessert. But instead of being fried, they are baked.

3 ripe bananas, peeled and chopped

2 ripe mangos, peeled, and chopped

12 fresh spring roll wrappers (or crêpes from the "Crêpes with Banana," page 133)

1 egg, whisked

1 Preheat the oven to 375°F.

2 In a bowl, gently mix the banana and mango, and divide into 12 equal portions. Take a wrapper or crêpe, and working with the side closest to you, add a fruit portion, spreading it lengthwise like a log. Fold the wrapper over the filling once, then fold in the sides, and roll almost to the end. Brush some egg wash on the inside of the wrapper, and finish rolling to the end to secure the filling. Repeat process until you have 12 spring rolls.

3 Place the spring rolls on a nonstick baking sheet, and place in the oven until golden and crispy all around, flipping once, about 15 minutes. Serve hot.

Calories 150	**Sodium** 50 mg	**EXCHANGES/ CHOICES**
Calories from Fat 10	**Potassium** 350 mg	1/2 Starch
Total Fat 1.0 g	**Total Carbohydrate** 35 g	2 Fruit
Saturated Fat 0.4 g	**Dietary Fiber** 3 g	
Trans Fat 0.0 g	**Sugars** 18 g	
Cholesterol 25 mg	**Protein** 3 g	

SUMMER PEACH SALAD WITH THAI BASIL

SERVES 6 | SERVING SIZE: 1 CUP

There are many wonderful ways to eat fruit. Curing fruit in vinegar is a great way to bring out their natural flavor and sweetness. Peaches or nectarines, tossed in balsamic vinegar or rice vinegar and garnished with fresh herbs such as Thai basil or mint, make a refreshing summer appetizer, salad, or snack. This recipe also works well with strawberries and plums.

6 peaches or nectarines, cut into 1/2-inch thick wedges, then halved crosswise

2 tablespoons aged balsamic or rice vinegar

6 large Thai basil or mint leaves, freshly torn

1 In a large bowl, toss the peaches with the vinegar.

2 Divide among 6 individual bowls or fruit cups. Garnish with basil or mint.

Calories 60	**Sodium** 0 mg
Calories from Fat 0	**Potassium** 285 mg
Total Fat 0.0 g	**Total Carbohydrate** 15 g
Saturated Fat 0.0 g	**Dietary Fiber** 2 g
Trans Fat 0.0 g	**Sugars** 13 g
Cholesterol 0 mg	**Protein** 1 g

EXCHANGES/ CHOICES
1 Fruit

STICKY RICE WITH MANGO AND COCONUT SAUCE

SERVES 8 | **SERVING SIZE: 1/3 CUP**

This Thai-inspired sticky rice and mango dessert is easy to make and requires only a handful of ingredients. The lemongrass-infused coconut sauce adds a creamy element and a flavor that is uniquely Southeast Asian.

1 cup light, unsweetened coconut milk

1 cup water

2 stalks lemongrass, trimmed, twisted, and knotted together

6 kaffir lime leaves (optional)

1 tablespoon agave nectar

1/2 teaspoon low-sodium salt

1 teaspoon tapioca starch or cornstarch diluted with 1 tablespoon water

2 1/2 cups white or black sticky rice, soaked overnight and drained

2 ripe mangos, peeled and sliced

6 to 12 fresh mint leaves

1 In a small pot, add the coconut milk, water, lemongrass, lime leaves, agave nectar, and salt, and bring to a gentle boil over medium heat. Reduce heat to low, and simmer for 20 minutes.

2 Whisk in the tapioca starch continuously until slightly thickened, about 1 minute.

3 Meanwhile, fill a wok halfway with water, set a steamer over the wok, and line it with cheesecloth. Spread the rice on top, cover with a lid, and steam over high heat for 20 minutes. Divide the rice among 8 plates, top with mango, and drizzle with coconut sauce. Garnish with mint. Serve at room temperature.

Calories 160	**Sodium** 60 mg	**EXCHANGES/ CHOICES**
Calories from Fat 20	**Potassium** 275 mg	2 Carbohydrate
Total Fat 2.0 g	**Total Carbohydrate** 33 g	1/2 Fat
Saturated Fat 1.6 g	**Dietary Fiber** 2 g	
Trans Fat 0.0 g	**Sugars** 10 g	
Cholesterol 0 mg	**Protein** 3 g	

CRÊPES WITH BANANA

SERVES 6 | SERVING SIZE: 1 CRÊPE

Crêpes are influenced by the French and first appeared in Southeast Asia in the mid 1800s. In Asia, coconut milk and rice flour replace the cow's milk and wheat flour, which give Asian crêpes a different flavor and texture. Serve in the afternoon as a snack with tea.

2 large eggs

1/3 cup rice flour

1 cup almond milk

1/4 cup grapeseed oil, divided use

3 ripe bananas, cut diagonally into 1/4-inch thick slices

6 large fresh mint leaves

1 In a medium bowl, whisk together the eggs, flour, and almond milk.

2 In a crêpe pan, melt 1 teaspoon grapeseed oil. Pour 1/3 cup batter into the pan. Cook on high, and allow it to set, about 1 minute. Flip and cook until golden, about 30 seconds. Slide onto plate and repeat 5 more times, until you have 6 crêpes.

3 Meanwhile, in a large nonstick pan, heat 1 tablespoon oil over medium heat. Place the banana slices in a single layer, and cook until golden on both sides, about 3 minutes. Divide the bananas into 6 portions, and fill each of the crêpes. Roll them up like cigars. Garnish with fresh mint and serve.

		EXCHANGES/ CHOICES
Calories 200	**Sodium** 55 mg	1/2 Starch
Calories from Fat 110	**Potassium** 290 mg	1 Fruit
Total Fat 12.0 g	**Total Carbohydrate** 22 g	2 Fat
Saturated Fat 1.5 g	**Dietary Fiber** 2 g	
Trans Fat 0.0 g	**Sugars** 8 g	
Cholesterol 60 mg	**Protein** 3 g	

ALMOND TAPIOCA WITH BANANA AND CORN

SERVES 16 | SERVING SIZE: 1/2 CUP

This almond milk-based tapioca is based on the classic coconut milk tapioca soup served throughout many parts of Asia, notably China, Vietnam, Cambodia, Thailand, Laos, and the Philippines, for example. This almond milk version is much lighter than the original, and is just as tasty. Top it with ripe banana or Roasted Tropical Bananas (page 138), sweet yellow corn, mango, sweet potato, or taro, or combination thereof, much like this popular banana and corn version.

8 cups unsweetened almond milk

1/3 cup tapioca pearls

3 tablespoons palm sugar or agave nectar

1/2 teaspoon low-sodium salt

2 ripe bananas, peeled and chopped

1 cup fresh or frozen sweet yellow corn kernels

Toasted sesame seeds

1 In a large pot, add the almond milk, and bring to a boil over high heat. Reduce heat to medium-low and add the pearls, stirring continuously to keep them separate. Add the palm sugar and salt and continue to cook until the pearls become fully transparent, about 30 minutes.

2 Turn off the heat, and stir in the bananas and corn. Serve garnished with toasted sesame seeds.

Calories 60	**Sodium** 115 mg
Calories from Fat 20	**Potassium** 225 mg
Total Fat 2.0 g	**Total Carbohydrate** 12 g
Saturated Fat 0.2 g	**Dietary Fiber** 1 g
Trans Fat 0.0 g	**Sugars** 5 g
Cholesterol 0 mg	**Protein** 1 g

EXCHANGES/ CHOICES
1 Carbohydrate

SPLIT YELLOW MUNG BEAN SOUP

SERVES 14 | SERVING SIZE: 1/2 CUP

Yellow split mung beans can be found in Asian or Indian markets. This sweet soup is best eaten hot and is perfect for serving as a snack during the cooler months of the year.

2 cups unsweetened light coconut milk

4 cups unsweetened rice milk

1 cup dried yellow split mung beans

2 tablespoons palm sugar or agave nectar

6 green cardamom pods (optional)

1/2 teaspoon low-sodium salt

3 teaspoons toasted sesame seeds

1 In a medium pot, add the coconut milk, rice milk, mung beans, agave nectar, cardamom (if using), and salt, and bring to a boil over medium heat.

2 Reduce heat to medium-low and cook, stirring occasionally, until the beans have broken down, and the soup is semi-smooth and lightly thickened, about 2 hours. Garnish lightly with toasted sesame seeds. Serve hot in individual bowls.

Calories 110	**Sodium** 55 mg
Calories from Fat 25	**Potassium** 300 mg
Total Fat 3.0 g	**Total Carbohydrate** 18 g
Saturated Fat 1.9 g	**Dietary Fiber** 4 g
Trans Fat 0.0 g	**Sugars** 7 g
Cholesterol 0 mg	**Protein** 5 g

EXCHANGES/ CHOICES
1 Carbohydrate
1/2 Fat

SWEET RED BEAN SOUP WITH CANDIED MANDARIN PEEL

SERVES 6 | SERVING SIZE: 1 CUP

Red bean soup is served during the Chinese New Year. The color red symbolizes "good luck." Adzuki beans can be found in Asian markets or health food stores, and sometimes even in the international food aisle of supermarkets. Candied mandarin peel can be made at home, but the more popular candied orange peels can be purchased and used here.

1 tablespoon palm sugar

3 mandarin peels, finely julienned

1 cup red adzuki beans, soaked in water overnight

2 tablespoons agave nectar

1/2 teaspoon salt

1 In a small pot, melt the palm sugar and mandarin peels over medium heat. Mix well and cook for 1 minute. Transfer to a plate, and separate each peel. Set aside until ready to use.

2 In a large pot, add 2 quarts water and beans, and bring to a boil over high heat. Reduce heat to medium-low, and cook until the beans have broken down and the soup has thickened, about 4 hours. Add the agave nectar and salt. Stir well and serve in individual bowls. Garnish lightly with some candied peels. Serve hot.

Calories 140	**Sodium** 200 mg
Calories from Fat 0	**Potassium** 415 mg
Total Fat 0.0 g	**Total Carbohydrate** 29 g
Saturated Fat 0.1 g	**Dietary Fiber** 4 g
Trans Fat 0.0 g	**Sugars** 7 g
Cholesterol 0 mg	**Protein** 7 g

EXCHANGES/ CHOICES
1 1/2 Starch
1/2 Carbohydrate

SWEET PUMPKIN SOUP

SERVES 6 | SERVING SIZE: 1 CUP

Sweet pumpkin soup is a favorite among many cultures. While classically it is made with coconut milk, rice milk is used in this recipe, allowing the sweet pumpkin flavor to shine.

1 kabocha pumpkin (about 2 1/2 lbs), peeled, seeded, and cut into 1-inch pieces

1 quart unsweetened, low-fat rice milk

1 quart filtered water

Sea salt, to taste

Freshly ground black pepper

1 In a medium pot, add the pumpkin, rice milk, and water, and bring to a boil over high heat. Reduce heat to low, and cook until the pumpkin pieces are tender, about 30 minutes. Let cool.

2 In a blender, process the pumpkin and cooking liquid until smooth. Pour mixture back into the pot. Season with salt and pepper to taste, and simmer until ready to serve.

Calories 120	**Sodium** 60 mg
Calories from Fat 10	**Potassium** 520 mg
Total Fat 1.0 g	**Total Carbohydrate** 28 g
Saturated Fat 0.0 g	**Dietary Fiber** 5 g
Trans Fat 0.0 g	**Sugars** 15 g
Cholesterol 0 mg	**Protein** 2 g

EXCHANGES/ CHOICES
2 Carbohydrate

ROASTED TROPICAL BANANAS

SERVES 6 | SERVING SIZE: 1 BANANA

The recipe is super simple. Turn on the oven, split the bananas in half lengthwise, and roast in their natural skins. It is amazing what you can do with just fruit. This dish is particularly wonderful on a cold winter night!

6 medium bananas, peel on, halved lengthwise

1 1/2 tablespoons melted salted butter

1 Preheat the oven to 400°F for 20 minutes.

2 On a large baking sheet, place the banana halves skin side down. Brush the top of each banana with the melted butter, and roast until golden and soft, about 10 minutes.

Calories 140	**Sodium** 25 mg	**EXCHANGES/ CHOICES**
Calories from Fat 30	**Potassium** 450 mg	2 Fruit
Total Fat 3.5 g	**Total Carbohydrate** 29 g	1/2 Fat
Saturated Fat 2.0 g	**Dietary Fiber** 3 g	
Trans Fat 0.1 g	**Sugars** 15 g	
Cholesterol 10 mg	**Protein** 1 g	

INDEX

BY SUBJECT

Note: Page numbers in **bold** indicate an
extensive discussion on the topic.